THE CHANGING ROOM

David Storey

D1635257

The Royal Court Writers Series published by

Royal Court Writers Series

The Changing Room was first published in Great Britain
by Jonathan Cape 1972, Penguin Books 1973
Published in the Royal Court Writers Series 1996
by Methuen Drama
an imprint of Reed International Books Ltd
Michelin House, 81 Fulham Road, London SW3 6RB
and Auckland, Melbourne, Singapore and Toronto
in association with the Royal Court Theatre
Sloane Square, London SW1N 8AS and
the Duke of York's Theatre, London
and distributed in the United States of America
by Heinemann, a division of Reed Elsevier Inc.
361 Hanover Street, Portsmouth, New Hampshire 03801 3959

Reprinted 1996

Copyright © 1972, 1996 by David Storey
The author has asserted his moral rights

ISBN 0 413 70370 3

A CIP catalogue record for this book
is available from the British Library

Front cover: Design by Oxygen

Typeset by Wilmaset Ltd, Birkenhead, Wirral
Printed and bound in Great Britain by
Cox & Wyman Ltd, Reading, Berkshire

Caution

Royal Court Theatre Productions Ltd
Duke of York's Theatre Ltd   The Theatre of Comedy Company
Dodger Productions
present
The Royal Court Classics Season

Stephen Bent Philip Martin Brown Brendan Coyle
Andrew Cryer Tim Dantay Chris Gascoyne
David Hargreaves Louis Hilyer Ewan Hooper
Alex McAvoy Nicholas McGaughey David MacCreedy
Jonathan Magnanti David Michaels Roger Morlidge
Roy North Jason Pitt Paul Rider Simon Rouse
Chris Walker Philip Whitchurch Simon Wolfe

The Changing Room

by **David Storey**

In association with **Theatre Royal, Plymouth**

Director **James Macdonald**
Designer **Hildegard Bechtler**
Costume Design **Ana Jebens**
Lighting Design **Rick Fisher**
Sound Design **Paul Arditti**

The Changing Room was first staged at the Royal Court Theatre on 9 November, 1971.
First performance of this production at the Duke of York's Theatre, as part of the
Royal Court Classics Season, 1 February, 1996.

The Duke of York's Theatre St Martin's Lane London WC2N 4BG
Sole Proprietor and Licensee The Duke of York's Theatre Ltd
Directors Sir Eddie Kulukundis OBE (Chairman) Howard Panter (Managing Director)
Peter Beckwith David Beresford Jones Robin Guilleret Rosemary Squire Miles Wilkin

Royal Court Theatre Productions Ltd Sloane Square London SW1W 8AS
Chairman John Mortimer CBE QC Artistic Director Stephen Daldry
General Manager Vikki Heywood Directors Stuart Burge CBE Anthony Burton
Graham Cowley Harriet Cruickshank Robert Fox Sonia Melchett Alan Rickman
Max Stafford-Clark James L Tanner

Season sponsored by
✦**Evening Standard**

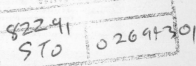

Royal Court Classics Season

Rufus Sewell in Ron Hutchinson's Rat in the Skull

Three plays from the extraordinary list of world-renowned playwrights to have been premiered over the past decades by the Royal Court are now presented at the Duke of York's Theatre in this first Season of Royal Court Classics.

This Season of landmark plays gives the Royal Court its third stage and a significant presence in the West End, and gives audiences the chance to experience three of the Royal Court's most celebrated successes.

The Classics Season began with a new production of Ron Hutchinson's *Rat in the Skull*, directed by Stephen Daldry, Artistic Director of the Royal Court, continued with the return of Phyllida Lloyd's production of Terry Johnson's hilarious hit *Hysteria* (winner of the 1994 Olivier Award for Best Comedy), before this new production of David Storey's epic *The Changing Room* directed by James Macdonald brings the Season to a close.

Duke of York's Box Office 0171 836 5122
Royal Court Box Office 0171 730 1745

The Producers of the Royal Court Classics Season wish to acknowledge financial support received from The Theatre Investment Fund, a registered charity, which invests in many commercial productions, runs seminars for new producers and raises money for commercial theatre. If you love the Theatre and wish to promote its future, please consider making a gift to the fund. For further information regarding the Fund and its activities, please contact:- Chief Executive, Theatre Investment Fund Limited, The Palace Theatre, Shaftesbury Avenue, London W1V 8AY. Telephone 0171 287 2144

What building has been more important to the culture of modern London - or indeed to modern drama anywhere? Since George Bernard Shaw challenged Edwardian Britain from the Royal Court, the theatre has been the brilliant bad boy of British drama, shocking and entertaining generations of Londoners.

It's the theatre we've always gone to for new ideas and new faces, to be in the know and to be outraged. For almost 40 years, since George Devine took Sloane Square in hand, if you didn't have a view on what was going on at the Court, you could hardly claim to be a theatregoing Londoner.

It's a unique London theatre not least because of its location, a wonderfully tatty building atop the tube line between stuffy Belgravia and the artificial Bohemia of the King's Road - an anachronistic yet peculiarly appropriate site. Not a Shaftesbury Avenue theatre but a crucial influence on the slower-thinking West End, as the dozens of successful transfers, from Arnold Wesker's *Roots* in 1959 to David Mamet's *Oleanna* in 1993 (both to the Duke of York's), have shown.

So why move into the West End? At the Evening Standard we think it is a brave and yet pragmatic move - and we have a long history of supporting such initiatives in the arts. It's the right move because the West End, stultified at the moment by commercial pressure and in fear of 'Broadwayisation', needs the Court - to remind it that theatre must challenge and thrill to survive. And the Court needs the West End - in these days no arts organisation can sit on its artistic integrity and allow others to exploit its successes. The Royal Court, with what I hope is just the first of many Classics Seasons, must remind us why we need theatre - and in doing so finance more work to rival what you will see here at the Duke of York's.

Stewart Steven

The Changing Room

by **David Storey** (1971)

Cast

Harry **Ewan Hooper**

Patsy **Chris Gascoyne**

Fielding **Chris Walker**

Mic Morley **Jonathan Magnanti**

Kendal **Brendan Coyle**

Luke **Paul Rider**

Fenchurch **Tim Dantay**

Colin Jagger **Louis Hilyer**

Trevor **David Michaels**

Walsh **Philip Whitchurch**

Sandford **Philip Martin Brown**

Barry Copley **David MacCreedy**

Jack Stringer **Simon Wolfe**

Bryan Atkinson **Roger Morlidge**

Billy Spencer **Andrew Cryer**

John Clegg **Stephen Bent**

Frank Moore **Jason Pitt**

Danny Crosby **Simon Rouse**

Cliff Owens **Nicholas McGaughey**

Tallon **Roy North**

Thornton **David Hargreaves**

Mackendrick **Alex McAvoy**

Understudy **Steve Jackson**

Director **James Macdonald**
Designer **Hildegard Bechtler**
Costume Design **Ana Jebens**
Lighting Design **Rick Fisher**
Sound Design **Paul Arditti**
Production Manager **Iain Gillie**
Company Stage Manager **Sheena Linden**
Deputy Stage Manager **Liz Thompson**
Assistant Stage Manager **Joan Coffey**
Costume Supervisor **Jennifer Cook**
Wardrobe Supervisor **Cathryn Johns**
Production Electrician **Jerry Hodgson**
Voice Coach **Julia Wilson-Dickson**
Assistant Director **Gordon Anderson**
Technical Advisor **Bev Risman**
Casting **Toby Whale**

There will be two intervals of fifteen minutes

Set built by **Robert Knight Ltd**
Set painted by **Derek Cowie**
Make up advisor **Rosemarie Swinfield**

Special thanks to **Halbro Sportswear Ltd** for team kit;
R E Webb of Gilberts for footwear and advice; to **Marsden
Weighing Machine Group Ltd** for the loan of the scales;
and to **Neil Mann** for the loan of the massage table.

The Company

David Storey (Writer)
For the Royal Court: The Restoration of Arnold Middleton (1967 Evening Standard Award for Most Promising Playwright), In Celebration (1969), The Contractor (1969; 1970 London Theatre Critics' Award for Best Play of the Year; named Writer of the Year by the Variety Club; 1973 New York Drama Critics' Award), Home (Evening Standard Drama Award; New York Drama Critics' Award), The Changing Room (1972 New York Drama Critics' Award), The Farm (1973), Life Class (1974), Mother's Day (1976).

For the Royal National Theatre: Early Days (1980), The March on Russia (1989; and UK tour under the title Jubilee), Stages.

Other plays include: Sisters (1978, Manchester Royal Exchange), Phoenix (1985, Century Theatre Company, Yorkshire).

Television plays includes: Home (1971), Grace (1974, adapted from a story by James Joyce).

Radio plays include: Stages, Caring (1994 BBC World Service).

Film screenplays include: This Sporting Life, In Celebration.

Novels include: This Sporting Life (1960 Macmillan Fiction Prize), Flight and Camden (1961 John Llewellyn Rhys Memorial Prize and 1963 Somerset Maugham Award), Pasmore (1973 Geoffrey Faber Memorial Prize), Saville (1976 Booker Prize).

David Storey was Assistant Artistic Director of the Royal Court, 1972-74.

Gordon Anderson (Assistant Director)
For 606 Theatre directed: The Grand Ceremonial (Lyric Studio), The Traitor (Bridewell Theatre), The Beggar's New Clothes (Cockpit Theatre and Broomhill Festival), The Honest Whore (Boulevard Theatre), Pantagleize (Canal Café Theatre).

Other theatre includes: The Lady of Pleasure (Cambridge University Marlowe Society at Cambridge Festival Theatre).

As an actor: Mad Forest (Royal Court and National Theatre of Romania), The Government Inspector, The Seagull, As You Like It (Sheffield Crucible Theatre), The Mysteries (Mermaid Theatre and tour of Portugal), Mongrel's Heart (Lyceum Theatre, Edinburgh).

Paul Arditti (Sound Designer)
For the Royal Court Classics Season: Hysteria, Rat in the Skull.

For the Royal Court: Bruises, Pale Horse, Not a Game for Boys, Mojo, Simpatico, The Steward of Christendom, The Strip, Uganda, The Knocky, Blasted, Peaches, The Editing Process, Babies, Some Voices, Thyestes, My Night with Reg, The Kitchen, The Madness of Esme and Shaz, Hammett's Apprentice, Hysteria, Live Like Pigs, Search and Destroy.

Other theatre sound design includes: Tartuffe (Manchester Royal Exchange); The Threepenny Opera (Donmar Warehouse); Hamlet (Gielgud); Piaf (Piccadilly); St Joan (Strand & Sydney Opera House); The Winter's Tale, Cymbeline, The Tempest, Antony & Cleopatra, The Trackers of Oxyrhynchus (Royal National Theatre); The Gift of the Gorgon (RSC and Wyndham's); Orpheus Descending (Theatre Royal, Haymarket, and Broadway); A Streetcar Named Desire (Bristol Old Vic), Tartuffe, The Winter's Tale (Manchester Royal Exchange); The Wild Duck (Phoenix); Henry IV, The Ride Down Mt Morgan (Wyndham's); Born Again (Chichester); Three Sisters, Matador (Queen's); Twelfth Night, The Rose Tattoo (Playhouse); Two Gentlemen of Verona, Becket, Cyrano de Bergerac (Theatre Royal, Haymarket); Travesties (Savoy); Four Baboons Adoring the Sun (Lincoln Center, 1992 Drama Desk Award).

Opera includes: Arianna, Gawain (ROH).
TV includes: The Camomile Lawn.

Hildegard Bechtler (Designer)
Theatre includes: Richard II (Royal National Theatre and Boubigny Paris), King Lear (Royal National Theatre and world tour), The Time and the Room (National Theatre, Madrid), St Pancras Project (LIFT), Footfalls (Garrick), Coriolanus (Salzburg Festival), Hedda Gabler (Abbey Theatre, Dublin and Playhouse London), Electra (Royal Shakespeare Company, Riverside Studios and Boubigny Paris).

Opera includes: Simon Boccanegra (Munich Staatsoper), Don Giovanni (Glyndebourne), Lohengrin, The Bacchae, Peter Grimes (ENO), Wozzeck, Don Carlos (Opera North), La Wally (Amsterdam

Musiktheatre and Bregenz Festival).

Television and films includes: Tx The Wasteland, Don Giovanni, Peter Grimes, Hedda Gabler, Echoes, The Works, How to Make a Flying Bird, Sacred Hearts, The Bad Sister, A Question of Choice, Business as Usual, Coming Up Roses.

Stephen Bent
For the Royal Court: Warren.

For the Royal National Theatre: The Ancient Mariner, Animal Farm, The Trackers of Oxyrhynchus (also at the Delphi Festival), Measure for Measure.

Other theatre includes: Grease (New London), The Night They Raided Minsky's (New Vic Co UK tour), Canterbury Tales (New Vic Co UK & USA tours), No Remission (Edinburgh Festival), Shooting Ducks (Edinburgh Festival and Stratford East), Richard III (Riverside Studios), Taming of the Shrew (Southampton and Rouen), Building Blocks (Windsor and Southampton), Rough Crossing (Southampton), Comedians, Threshold (Lyric, Belfast).

Television includes: BBC Screen 2's Lovebirds, Sweet Nothings, Close Relations, BBC comedy series Down to Earth, The Bill, Casualty, Miss Marple A Caribbean Mystery, For Valour: The John Phillips Story.

Films include: The Fourth Protocol, McVicar, Who Dares Wins, Those Glory Glory Days.

Philip Martin Brown
Theatre includes: Two (WYP), Anyone for Dennis (West End), Roll on Four O'Clock, Loot (Lyric), Chips with Everything (Birmingham Rep).

Television includes: The Six Sides of Coogan, Men of the World, Into the Fire, Band of Gold, Lifeboat, Between the Lines, Heartbeat, Birds of a Feather, Young Indiana Jones, Chronicles, Die Kinder, Sharp End, The Chain, The Paradise Club, 1914 All Out, A Perfect Spy, The Monocled Mutineer, Bluebell, Bull Week, Enemy at the Door, A Horseman Riding By.

Film includes: Coming Through, Eye of the Needle, Bounty, Party Party.

Brendan Coyle
For the Royal Court: Pygmies in the Ruins (from Lyric Theatre, Belfast).

Other theatre includes: Playboy of the Western World, Over the Bridge, All Souls Night (Lyric Theatre, Belfast), The Ragged Trousered Philanthropists (UK tour), The Plough and the Stars (UK and Eire tours), Elegies (King's Head and Drill Hall), Judgement Day (Old Red Lion), September Tide (King's Head and Comedy), Philadelphia Here I Come (King's Head and Wyndham's), The Love Song for Ulster Trilogy (Tricycle Theatre), The Silver Tassie (Almeida), Force and Hypocrisy (Young Vic).

Television includes: The Glass Virgin, Dangerfield, The Full Wax, The Bill, London Calling, Silent Witness, Thieftakers.

Film includes: Ailsa.

Andrew Cryer
For the Royal Shakespeare Company: King Lear, The Last Days of Don Juan, The Pretenders, The Taming of the Shrew, As You Like It, The Merry Wives of Windsor, Antony and Cleopatra.

Other theatre includes: South Pacific, Sinbad (Queen's Theatre, Hornchurch), A Midsummer Night's Dream, Antony and Cleopatra (Northern Broadsides), The Cracked Pot (West Yorkshire Playhouse), The Winslow Boy (Scarborough Theatre in the Round).

Television includes: The Bill, Peak Practice.

Tim Dantay
Theatre includes: Lonely Hearts, Off Out (Hull Truck Theatre Company), Bent (Expressions Studio, Manchester), Billy's Last Stand (Liverpool Playhouse), Soft (Contact Theatre, Manchester), Orphans, Mistress of the Inn, Strippers, (Mercury Theatre, Colchester), Loot (Coliseum Theatre, Oldham).

Television includes: Making Out (three series), The Bill, British Slaves, Go Back Out ...., Peak Practice, Pie in the Sky, Common as Muck, Cardiac Arrest, Casualty, Heartbeat, EastEnders.

Films include: Road, Starlings.

Rick Fisher (Lighting Designer)
For the Royal Court Classics Season: Hysteria, Rat in the Skull.

For the Royal Court: The Queen & I, Hysteria, King Lear, Six Degrees of Separation (also West End), Three Birds Alighting on a Field, Bloody Poetry, Serious Money (also West End and Broadway), A Mouthful of Birds.

Other recent theatre includes: Macbeth

(Greenwich); An Inspector Calls (RNT, Aldwych, Broadway, Tokyo, Australia, Garrick); Under Milk Wood, What the Butler Saw, Pericles, Machinal (RNT); Something About Us (Lyric Studio, Hammersmith); The Threepenny Opera, The Life of Stuff (Donmar Warehouse); The Cryptogram (Ambassadors); Much Ado About Nothing (Queen's); The Blue Macushla (Druid Galway); The Gift of the Gorgon (RSC and Wyndham's).

Opera includes: Fairy Queen (ENO); Cosi Fan Tutte (WNO); The Magic Flute (Parma); Gloriana, La boheme, L'Etoile, Peter Grimes (Opera North); Manon Lescaut (Dublin); and three seasons of outdoor operas in Batignano, Italy.

Dance includes: Swan Lake (AMP at Sadler's Wells).

Received nominations for Olivier Awards in 1995 and 1993. In 1994 won the Olivier Award for his work on Machinal, Moonlight and Hysteria; and the Tony and Drama Desk Awards for the Broadway production of An Inspector Calls. Is currently Chairman of the Association of Lighting Designers.

Chris Gascoyne
For the Royal National Theatre: Racing Demon, Murmuring Judges.

Other theatre includes: Ya Shunta Joined (Nottingham Playhouse), The Long and The Short and The Tall (Man in the Moon).

Television includes: The Bill, Casualty, Hard Cases, The Secret Diary of Adrian Mole, The Growing Pains of Adrian Mole, Frontiers, Peak Practice, Between The Lines.

Films: Suckers.

David Hargreaves
Theatre includes: Subject for Interrogation, Wednesday, Devour the Snow (Bush), Landscape of Exile (Foco Novo), It's a Mad House (Leeds), The Best Girl in Ten Streets (Soho Poly), A Passion in Six Days (Sheffield Crucible), A View from the Bridge (Young Vic), Happy Jack (tour), The Father (Farnham Redgrave), The Doll's House (Riverside), Chekhov's Women (Lyric Hammersmith), Is This The Day?, A View from the Bridge (Northampton), Twelfth Night (tour and Playhouse), Raising Hell (Inner City Theatre Co), A Passionate Woman (West Yorkshire Playhouse), Casement, Bierdeman and the Fireraisers (Moving Theatre at the Riverside), Antony and Cleopatra (Moving Theatre tour).

Television includes: The XYZ Man, Armchair Thriller, The Strangers, Stronger than the Sun, The House of Caradus, Sally Ann, A Leap in the Dark, The Professionals, Minor Complications, Together, Juliet Bravo, Sorry I'm a Stranger Here Myself, Science Workshop, Forever Young, The Intercession, A Brother's Tale, Mistress Masham's Repose, Bulman, The Seagreen Man, Shine on Harvey Moon, Albion Market, 1914 All Out, Closing Ranks, Truckers, The Place of Safety, Erasmus Microman, No Further Cause for Concern, Casualty, Making Out, Thatcher - The Final Days, Hard Cases, Saracen, She's Been Away, All Creatures Great and Small, Poirot, Madly in Love, The Miners' Strike, Tecx, The Conversion of St Paul, Kingdom Come, Keeper, Woof, Josie, Heartbeat, Inspector Alleyn Death at the Bar, The Mendip Mystery, The Tempest, The Bill, Justice for Gemma, Harry, Ruth Rendell: Vanity Dies Hard, Earthfasts, Peak Practice, Hetty Wainthropp Investigates, Some Kind of Life, Expert Witness.

Radio includes: Bright Days, The High Frontier, Sleeping Dogs Lie.

Louis Hilyer
For the Royal National Theatre: An Inspector Calls (and Aldwych Theatre and world tour).

For the Royal Shakespeare Company: Les Liasons Dangeureuses (Ambassadors Theatre).

Other theatre includes: The Great Pretenders, Bad Blood (Gate Theatre), The Beaux Stratagem (English Touring Theatre), Hamlet (Actors Touring Company), Edward II, The Alchemist (Royal Exchange, Manchester), Loot (Bristol Old Vic), Beggars Opera (Belgrade, Coventry), French Without Tears (Palace Theatre, Watford).

Television includes: Brookside, The Free Frenchman, Alas Smith and Jones, Press Gang, Zorro, Minder, The Bill, Between the Lines, Absolutely Fabulous, Degas and Pissarro Fall Out for Without Walls.

Ewan Hooper
For the Royal Court: Bingo, Falkland Sound/Gibraltar Strait, All Things Nice, Hammett's Apprentice, The Kitchen.

For the Royal National Theatre: Roots.

For the Royal Shakespeare Company:

Henry V, Coriolanus, Broken Heart.

Other theatre includes: Rutherford and Son (New End), Hippolytyos, Hard Heart (Almeida), She Stoops to Conquer, Doctor's Dilemma, The Recruiting Officer, Richard II (Manchester Royal Exchange).

Television includes: Hunters Walk, King Lear, Invasion, Across the Lake, Roots.

Films include: Dracula Has Risen From the Grave, How I Won the War, Julius Caesar, Personal Services.

Ana Jebens (Costume Designer)

Theatre includes: The Robbers, Penthesilea (Hamburg) and for the Swan, Worcester, the Half Moon and Bush Theatres.

TV includes: Burning Embers (Channel 4), Killing Time.

Opera includes: Passion Killers (Mecklenburgh Opera).

Alex McAvoy

Theatre includes: Joseph and the Amazing Technicolor Dreamcoat (West End), The Plough and the Stars (Citizens' Theatre, Glasgow), Othello (Royal Lyceum Theatre, Edinburgh), Comedy of Errors (Young Vic and Edinburgh Festival), Romeo and Juliet, Bible One (Young Vic), The Three Estaites (Scottish Theatre Company for Edinburgh and Warsaw Festivals), The Ragged Trousered Philanthropists, In Time of Strife (7:84), Habeas Corpus (Birmingham Stage Company), The Taming of the Shrew, Make a Break, Habeas Corpus (national tours), Cinderella (Gaiety Theatre, Ayr), Dick Whittington (King's Theatre, Edinburgh), Passing By (Old Red Lion). Also studied mime under Jacques Lecoq in Paris.

Television includes: Dad's Army, Z Cars , The Bill, Minder, Julie Felix Show, Tessie O'Shea Show, Square Mile of Murder, House with the Green Shutters, The Vital Spark, A Matter of Expression, Tucker's Luck, Portrait of Isa Mulvaney, Down Where the Buffalo Go, Variations, Dialogue in the Dark.

Films include: You're Only Young Twice, VIP, Country Dance, The Day of the Otter, Pink Floyd-The Wall, Pink Floyd-The Final Cut, The Monkey's Paw, Venus Peter.

Nicholas McGaughey

Royal National Theatre includes: Under Milk Wood.

Other theatre includes: Macbeth (WNO),

The History of Mr Polly (Torch).

Television includes: Sharpe's Gold, Mind to Kill, Excalibur, Lifeboat, Judas and the Gimp, Sticky Wickets, Tell Tale, The Whistling Boy.

Films include: The Englishman Who Went Up A Hill, The Proposition, Wild Justice, Bad Company.

Radio includes: The Mabinogi.

David MacCreedy

For the Royal Court: Mad Forest (also at the National Theatre, Bucharest).

Other theatre includes: Passion Killers (Hull Truck), The End of the Food Chain (Scarborough), Imagine Drowning (Hampstead).

Television includes: Preston Front, Heartbeat, Our Friends in the North, The Cinder Path, All Quiet on the Preston Front, The Wanderer, Hetty Wainthropp Investigates, Crime Unlimited, In Suspicious Circumstances, Spender, Calling the Shots, Rumpole of the Bailey, Sam Saturday, A Likely Lad, A Time to Dance.

Films include: Captives.

James Macdonald (Director)

For the Royal Court: Simpatico, Blasted, Peaches, Thyestes, Putting Two and Two Together, The Terrible Voice of Satan, Hammett's Apprentice.

Other theatre includes: Love's Labours Lost, Richard II (Manchester Royal Exchange), The Rivals (Nottingham Playhouse), The Crackwalker (Gate), The Seagull (Sheffield Crucible), Neon Gravy (RNT Studio), Miss Julie (Oldham Coliseum), Juno and the Paycock, Ice Cream and Hot Fudge, Romeo and Juliet, Fool for Love and Savage/Love, Master Harold and the Boys (Contact Theatre), Lives of the Great Poisoners (Second Stride, Riverside), Prem (BAC, Soho Poly), Good Person of Szechwan, The Dragon (I Gelati Theatre Company).

Jonathan Magnanti

Theatre includes: The Brothers Karamazov (Manchester Royal Exchange), The Unexpected Guest (Plymouth Theatre Royal), Only Playing Miss (Neti Neti Theatre Co), Absent Friends (English Theatre of Hamburg).

Television includes: Boon, Split Ends, The Saint, Poirot, A Guilty Thing Surprised, Heartbeat, In Suspicious

Circumstances, Anna Lee, The Bill, A
Terrible Coldness, Brighton Boy, Finney,
Lovejoy, The Chief, Band of Gold,
Emmerdale, Tomorrow's World,
Cardiac Arrest.

David Michaels

For the Royal National Theatre: Fuente
Ovejuna.

Other theatre includes: The Winter's
Tale, A Midsummer Night's Dream, Babes
in Arms (New Shakespeare Company);
Holidays (West Yorkshire Playhouse);
East Lynne (Farnham), Return of the
Native (Worcester), A Taste of Honey
(Nottingham), Twelfth Night, Hamlet (UK
tours); Shakespeare's Lovers, God Say
Amen (US tours).

Television includes: Peak Practice,
Coronation Street, Money for Nothing,
Bambino Mio, The Bill, Soldier Soldier,
The Water Babies, The Sword and the
Circle, Inspector Morse, How We Used
To Live, Crown Court, The Family.

Films include: Frank's Bits, Misterioso,
A Better Life Than Mine.

Roger Morlidge

For the Royal Court: Wildfire (Young
People's Theatre tour).

Other theatre includes: Blue
Remembered Hills (Sheffield Crucible),
Peter Pan (Birmingham Rep), Under Milk
Wood (Wimbledon Studio Theatre).

Television includes: Six Sides of Coogan,
Hetty Wainthropp Investigates, Pie in the
Sky, Frontiers, Band of Gold, The Bill,
EastEnders.

Film includes: The English Patient.

Roy North

Theatres includes: Robert and Elizabeth,
Canterbury Tales, Joseph and the Amazing
Technicolor Dreamcoat (all in the West End),
Hair (Amsterdam), Whodunnit, The
Haunting of Hill House, Alphabetical Order,
Move Over Mrs Markham, Candida, Touch
and Go, How the Other Half Loves,
Charley's Aunt and Noises Off (all tours),
Richard III, A Midsummer Night's Dream,
Antony and Cleopatra, The Merry Wives
(Northern Broadstairs Company) and in
repertory at Southwold, Harrogate, Hull
and Leeds.

Television includes: Heartbeat, The Bill,
Shoestring, The Brack Report, The Kenny
Everett Show, Bergerac, Colin's Sandwich,
and presented The Basil Brush Show

and Get It Together.

Radio includes: Richard III.

Jason Pitt

Theatre includes: Home (national tour
and Wyndham's Theatre), The Milk Train
Doesn't Stop Here Anymore (Glasgow
Citizens Theatre), Border Crossing
(Salisbury Playhouse), The Butcher of
Bagdhad (Cherub Theatre Company at
The Latchmere), Sex and Violence at the
Fantasy Café (Edinburgh Festival), The
Comedy of Errors, Success Story
(Whitehorse Theatre Company).

Television includes: Strike Force, The
Outrage, The Famous Five, The Bill.

Paul Rider

Theatre includes: Bouncers, Up 'N' Under,
Teechers, Twelfth Night (Hull Truck Theatre
Company in the West End), On the Piste
(Hull Truck Theatre Company), Edward II,
Hamlet (Compass Theatre Company,
Sheffield), A Midsummer Night's Dream,
She Stoops to Conquer, Flarepath (Bristol
Old Vic), Savages, Lucky Sods (West
Yorkshire Playhouse), Richard II, East
(Oldham Coliseum), The Plough and the
Stars (Leicester Haymarket).

Television includes: The Ritz, Who's Line
is it Anyway?, The Bill, The Continental,
Bare Necessities.

Bev Risman (Technical Advisor)

Born in Salford, Manchester, and grew up
in the Lake District. He first signed for
Leigh, near Wigan, in Lancashire before
transferring to Leeds Rugby Football Club.
He was the Leeds full back in the famous
'water splash' cup final in 1968. He has
played for England at Rugby Union, and for
England and Great Britain at Rugby
League, captaining both. Bev has been
involved in the development of Rugby
League in London for some years and is
co-ordinator for student Rugby League in
this country, organising student World
Cups both in England and Australia. He is
currently organising another World Cup
to be held here in August of this year.

Bev was technical advisor on the
original production of The Changing
Room in 1971.

Simon Rouse

For the Royal Court: The Sea, Runaway.

For the Royal Shakespeare Company:
Coriolanus, Antony and Cleopatra, Titus

Andronicus, 'Tis Pity She's a Whore, Lorenzaccio, Sons of Light.

Other theatre includes: Sweet Bird of Youth (Theatre Royal, Haymarket); The Caretaker (Shaw); The Looneys (Hampstead); Fishing, Lenz (New End); Ghosts, The Way of the World, Rat in the Skull (tours).

Television includes: The Bill, Free as a Bird, Wednesday Love, Sam, Softly Softly, Marked Personal, Kipper, Dead Shepherd, C.A.T.S. Eyes, Operation Julie, One Bummer News Day, Crime and Punishment, Even Solomon, St Joan, Sheppey, Dr Who, Cricket, Billy Liar, The Brief, Portrait in Black, You Never Get What You Want, Crown Court, Juliet Bravo, Robin of Sherwood, The Practice, Bread, The Master Builder, Hard Cases, A Ticket to Ride, Here is the News, Tecx, Casualty, Wilderness Edge, Minder, Dead Romantic.

Films include: The Ragman's Daughter, Butley, White Bird, Dick Turpin, The Professionals, Smuggler, The Manions of America, Retribution, The Cure, Blood Royal, Bones, Operation Julie, The Saint.

Chris Walker

For the Royal National Theatre: Richard III (USA Tour).

Theatre includes: Up 'N' Under, Bouncers, Cramp (Hull Truck Theatre Company Tours and West End), Salt of the Earth (Hull Truck Tour and New York Festival).

Television includes: Our Friends in the North, Class Act, Heartbeat V, Danger in Mind, The Manageress (two series), The Bill (two series), Breed of Heroes, Harry, Peak Practice, Poirot.

Films include: When Saturday Comes (not yet released), The Fourth Protocol, Funny Man.

Philip Whitchurch

For the Royal Court: Keeping Body and Soul Together.

For the Royal National Theatre: Women of Troy.

Other theatre includes: Othello, The Knickers (Lyric, Hammersmith), The Crucible (Manchester Royal Exchange), Pravda (Nottingham Playhouse), A Midsummer Night's Dream, Don Juan, Rat in the Skull (Sheffield Crucible), Widowing of Mrs Holroyd (Leicester Haymarket), Waiting for Godot (Coventry Belgrade), The Alchemist (Cambridge Theatre

Company), The Doll's House (Oxford Touring), Widower's Houses, A Month in the Country (Palace Watford).

Television includes: The Brothers McGregor, Casualty, Boon, Coronation Street, Sharpe's Enemy, The Detectives, The Bill, Sharpe's Seige, GBH.

As a writer: adapted La Bete Humaine (Nottingham Playhouse), In the Midnight Hour (national tour and Young Vic), Face (co-written with Bob Carlton).

Simon Wolfe

For the Royal National Theatre: At Our Table.

Other theatre includes: The Traitor (606 Theatre Company at the Bridewell), Hereward the Wake (Wolsey Theatre, Ipswich, and tour), The Corsican Brothers (Abbey Theatre, Dublin), Volpone (Almeida)

Television includes: The Great Kandinsky, The Bill.

Royal Court Theatre Productions Ltd
(Co-Producer)

Was formed to expand the work of the English Stage Company in the West End, with any profits covenanted to support the work at Sloane Square.

Its first transfer was Caryl Churchill's Serious Money to the Wyndham's in 1987, followed by Timberlake Wertenbaker's Our Country's Good to the Garrick in 1989, Ariel Dorfman's Death and the Maiden to the Duke of York's in 1992, Six Degrees of Separation by John Guare to the Comedy, also in 1992, and David Mamet's Oleanna again to the Duke of York's, and Kevin Elyot's My Night With Reg to the Criterion, both in 1994.

Dodger Productions (Co-Producer)

Is a theatrical partnership comprising Michael David, Doug Johnson, Rocco Landesman, Des McAnuff, Edward Strong and Sherman Warner, who work together in various combinations. Originating at New York's Brooklyn Academy of Music in 1978, the Dodgers produced Gimme Shelter, Holeville, Emigres and The Bread and Puppet Theatre before migrating to the New York Shakespeare Festival, where they produced Mary Stuart and How it All Began.

On Broadway, some of the award-winning productions for which they have been responsible are: Hamlet starring Ralph

Fiennes with the Almeida, The Who's Tommy, Alan Menken's A Christmas Carol, Guys and Dolls directed by Jerry Zaks, The Secret Garden, Jelly's Last Jam, Craig Lucas' Prelude to a Kiss, Roger Miller's Big River, Stephen Sondheim's Into the Woods, Pumpboys and Dinettes and The Gospel at Colonus. Current productions on Broadway are How to Succeed in Business Without Really Trying starring Matthew Broderick, directed by Des McAnuff, the upcoming new productions of Stephen Sondheim's A Funny Thing Happened on the Way to the Forum and Rodgers and Hammerstein's The King and I, and Disney's Beauty and the Beast which opened in April, 1994 (for which they provide general management).

David Strong Warner, Inc is the management company that administers Dodger Productions. D Tours is an affiliate company which books and markets touring attractions. Another related company of the Dodgers restored and now operates the Goldenrod Showboat, a national landmark, in St Charles, Missouri.

The Duke of York's Theatre Ltd
(Co-Producer) in conjunction with the Turnstyle Group Ltd
Award-winning plays presented at the Duke of York's Theatre under the current management include the Royal Court Theatre's productions of Ariel Dorfman's Death and the Maiden and David Mamet's Oleanna, directed by Harold Pinter; Jonathan Harvey's Beautiful Thing; and the Royal National Theatre's production of Arthur Miller's Broken Glass.

The Turnstyle Group's recent productions include the multi award-winning West End premiere of Oscar Hammerstein II's Carmen Jones, directed by Simon Callow at The Old Vic and on UK and Japanese tours; Jonathan Harvey's award-winning comedy Beautiful Thing; A Slip of the Tongue starring John Malkovich; Shades starring Pauline Collins; Single Spies, the award-winning double bill by Alan Bennett, starring Simon Callow, Prunella Scales and Alan Bennett himself; Frankie and Johnny in the Clair de Lune starring Julie Walters and Brian Cox; Look Back in Anger with Kenneth Branagh and Emma Thompson; the Renaissance Theatre Company's Shakespeare season starring Kenneth Branagh and directed by Dame Judi Dench, Geraldine McEwan and Sir Derek Jacobi;

The Common Pursuit by Simon Gray starring Stephen Fry, Rik Mayall and John Sessions; and When I Was a Girl I Used to Scream and Shout starring Julie Walters and Geraldine James.

The Theatre of Comedy Company
(Co-Producer)
The Theatre of Comedy Company Limited, which was formed by Ray Cooney in 1983 with some 30 actors and writers, has produced a wide variety of productions since its first smash hit with Ray Cooney's Run for Your Wife way back in 1983. They include Peter O'Toole in Shaw's Pygmalion, Alan Ayckbourn's marathon two-hander sequence Intimate Exchanges, See How They Run (winning Founder-Member Maureen Lipman an Olivier Award), Peter Nichols's Passion Play and Priestley's When We Are Married (winning Olivier Awards for Best Comedy Performance - Bill Fraser - and Best Comedy Production). After a period of concentration on the refurbishment of the Shaftesbury (of which the Company owns the freehold), the Company returned to active production in splendid style with Ray Cooney's Out of Order, which won the Olivier Comedy of the Year Award for 1991. This production had a long and successful tour.

The Company's recent West End productions have been John Guare's Six Degrees of Separation (in a co-production with the Royal Court) which won the Olivier Award for the Best Play of 1993 and the critically acclaimed Hay Fever at the Albery Theatre. They also produced a successful tour of John Godber's Happy Families. The Company has collaborated several times with the Royal Court, including the first production of Hysteria. The Company's most recent production was The Prime of Miss Jean Brodie starring Patricia Hodge at the Strand Theatre. Recently the Company took over the management of the Churchill, Bromley and a recent production of Hot Mikado transferred to the Queen's Theatre.

The Company co-produces the very popular TV series As Time Goes By starring founder members Dame Judi Dench and Geoffrey Palmer. The Company also co-produced a new four part series Love on a Branch Line which was screened in June 1994 on BBC TV.

Royal National Theatre

Rosencrantz and Guildenstern are Dead

by Tom Stoppard

Adrian Scarborough, Alan Howard & Simon Russell Beale. Photo: Robert Workman

"Matthew Francis's sumptuously staged new production" Evening Standard

"Superb performances from **Simon Russell Beale** and **Adrian Scarborough"**
Daily Telegraph

"Alan Howard in full theatrical flood"
Evening Standard

"Exuberantly funny" Guardian

"DAZZLING REVIVAL" Sunday Times

NT
ROYAL
NATIONAL
THEATRE

Box Office 0171-928 2252
First Call 0171-420 0000
Now in repertoire in the Lyttelton

Reg'd Charity

THE ARTS COUNCIL OF ENGLAND

N. CHARLESWORTH 1990

The Duke of York's Theatre

The theatre, which opened on 10 September 1892 with The Wedding Eve, was built for Frank Wyatt and his wife, Violet Melnotte. Initially called the Trafalgar Square, the name was shortened to Trafalgar in 1894, and the following year became the Duke of York's to honour the future King George V. Violet Melnotte owned the theatre for the rest of her life, often leasing it to other managements, mostly - notably in its early history - to Charles Frohman. The first long run under his aegis was Anthony Hope's The Adventures of Lady Ursula. In 1900 Jerome K Jerome's Miss Hobbs was staged on the same bill as a one-act play by David Belasco, a friend of Frohman's. It was entitled Madame Butterfly and, purely by chance, was seen by Puccini who later turned it into what is probably his most famous opera; as such it was ultimately performed at the Duke of York's in 1932 by the Carl Rosa Opera Company.

The theatre's association with J M Barrie began in 1902 with the presentation of The Admirable Crichton. However, the most endearing production arising from this relationship was Peter Pan, first seen in 1904 and revived every Christmas until 1915. The last of Barrie's important works to have its debut at the Duke of York's was What Every Woman Knows, in 1908.

During Frohman's management period there were occasional limited seasons featuring special guest stars, including Isadora Duncan, Sarah Bernhardt, Yvette Guilbert and Albert Chevalier. From February to June 1910, Frohman put on an ambitious repertory season of ten plays - some revivals, some new. Most noteworthy of the untried productions were Galsworthy's Justice, Granville Barker's The Madras House and Shaw's Misalliance.

After Frohman died in 1915, aboard the torpedoed liner Lusitania, another repertory company, Miss Horniman's from the Gaiety, Manchester, took over for a season which included Hindle Wakes by Stanley Houghton. The big money-spinners of the First World War years were Romance, Daddy Long Legs and The Thirteenth Chair in which Mrs Patrick Campbell played Rosalie La Grange. Two considerable successes of the 1920s were revues: The Punch Bowl and London Calling, the latter largely written by Noël Coward. His Easy Virtue starring Jane Cowl, Joyce Carey and Adrianne Allen attracted full houses during 1926 - although his Home Chat the following year did not. Matheson Lang presented and appeared in a number of dramas towards the end of the decade. These included Jew Süss which gave Peggy Ashcroft her first important role in the West End.

The 1930s brought a number of interesting seasons, amongst them The Carl Rosa Opera Company, Grand Guignol, Nancy Price's People's National Theatre, The Ballet Rambert and the notable appearances of Markova and Dolin which greatly helped to popularise ballet in England. Apart from these, a very successful play in 1931 was John van Druten's London Wall in which John Mills scored a great personal triumph.

During the Second World War Is Your Honeymoon Really Necessary? which opened in 1944 enjoyed a two-year run. Subsequently, a pair of peace-time revues,

One Two Three and Four Five Six, starring Binnie Hale, Sonnie Hale and Bobby Howes, played for over twelve months. In the early 1950s John Clements and Kay Hammond achieved an enormous success with The Happy Marriage. Anouilh's Point of Departure, starring Mai Zetterling and Dirk Bogarde, who gave a widely-acclaimed performance, was also staged during this period and Orson Welles' adaptation of Moby Dick, with Joan Plowright, ran for a limited season in 1955. A year later, Hugh Mills' The House By the Lake, starring Flora Robson, played for over 700 performances.

Notable productions during the 1960s include: the revue One Over the Eight with Kenneth Williams and Sheila Hancock, Frank Marcus' The Killing of Sister George, with Beryl Reid and Eileen Atkins, and Alan Ayckbourn's Relatively Speaking, which starred Celia Johnson, Michael Hordern, Richard Briers and Jennifer Hilary.

The following decade started with a two-and-a-half year run of The Man Most Likely To and ended with two distinguished productions - Half Life which was transferred from the National Theatre with John Gielgud in the leading role, and Clouds which paired Tom Courtenay and Felicity Kendal, previously presented at the Hampstead Theatre Club. During the run of Clouds, Capital Radio purchased the freehold of the Duke of York's from Peter Saunders, its then owner, closing it in May 1979 for complete refurbishment, including the removal of a number of pillars from the auditorium.

On 10 February 1980 there was a reopening Gala in aid of the Combined Theatrical Charities at which fifty stars gave their services in a performance reflecting the history of The Duke of York's.

The first production under the aegis of Capital Radio was Rose starring Glenda Jackson, which played to near-capacity business from February to August 1980. The award-winning Duet For One by Tom Kempinski, with Frances de la Tour and David de Keyser, was followed by other successes, including J P Donleavy's The Beastly Beatitudes of Balthazar B, Donald Sinden and Beryl Reid in The School For Scandal, and Al Pacino's award-winning performance in David Mamet's American Buffalo. Richard Harris' comedy Stepping

Out, directed by Julia Mackenzie, ran for almost three years to be succeeded by the acclaimed revival of Alan Ayckbourn's comedy How the Other Half Loves and Tom Stoppard's Artist Descending a Staircase. In June 1989 Willy Russell's Shirley Valentine opened at the Duke of York's, this time with Hannah Gordon, and ran for over two years. The next production was another one-woman show, Dickens' Women, written by and starring Miriam Margolyes, which transferred from the Hampstead Theatre. Two short seasons brought 1991 to a close; they were Stephen Mallatratt's The Glory in the Garden and Sheridan Morley's Noël and Gertie.

In March 1992 the Duke of York's Theatre was bought from Capital Radio by a consortium whose directors are Sir Eddie Kulukundis OBE, Howard Panter, Peter Beckwith, David Beresford Jones and Robin Guilleret. This coincided with London's hottest ticket - the Royal Court's production of Ariel Dorfman's Death and the Maiden which won awards for both the author and Juliet Stephenson's electrifying performance. Roald Dahl's The Witches followed for a highly successful Christmas season.

The Young Vic's production of Arthur Miller's The Last Yankee transferred in 1993 to great acclaim. The Royal Court followed, in September, with another sell-out season. This time it was David Mamet's Oleanna, starring David Suchet and Lia Williams, which took us into June 1994. A long hot summer was made even hotter by Richard O'Brien's The Rocky Horror Show making a pit stop on its 21st Birthday celebratory national tour - tickets were like gold dust. A season with award-winning playwright Jonathan Harvey's Beautiful Thing and a transfer from the National Theatre of Arthur Miller's latest, award-winning play, Broken Glass, brought us back to The Rocky Horror Show in May 1995.

Assistance in the preparation of this article is gratefully acknowledged to Geoffrey Ashton's History of the Duke of York's Theatre.

How the Royal Court is brought to you

The English Stage Company at the Royal Court Theatre is supported financially by a wide range of public bodies and private companies, as well as its own trading activities. The theatre receives its principal funding from the **Arts Council of England**, which has supported the Royal Court since 1956. **The Royal Borough of Kensington & Chelsea** gives an annual grant to the Royal Court Young People's Theatre and provides some of its staff. The **London Boroughs Grants Committee** contributes to the cost of productions in the Theatre Upstairs.

Other parts of the Royal Court's activities are made possible by business sponsorships. Several of these sponsors have made a long term commitment. 1995 saw the fifth Barclays New Stages Festival of Independent Theatre, which has been supported throughout by **Barclays Bank**. **British Gas North Thames** supported three years of the Royal Court's Education Programme. Sponsorship by **WH Smith** helped make the launch of the Friends of the Royal Court scheme so successful.

1993 saw the start of our association with the **Audrey Skirball-Kenis Theatre**, of Los Angeles. The Skirball Foundation is funding a Playwrights Programme at the Royal Court. Exchange visits for writers between Britain and the USA complement the greatly increased programme of readings and workshops which have fortified the Royal Court's capability to develop new plays. The vital support of **The Jerwood Foundation** has helped produce these plays, many of them by first time writers.

The Royal Court earns the rest of the money it needs to operate from the Box Office, from other trading and from the transfers of plays such as *Death and the Maiden*, *Six Degrees of Separation*, *Oleanna* and *My Night With Reg* to the West End. But without public subsidy it would close immediately and its unique place in British Theatre would be lost.

The Royal Court Theatre has recently received the news that it has been awarded a much needed grant of just under £16 million from the **Arts Council**, to refurbuish and develop its unique property in Sloane Square, ensuring the theatre's survival well into the next century.

The application to the **Arts Council** for this award would not have been possible without the efforts and support of the recent **Olivier Appeal** which enabled the Royal Court to begin repairs and improvements to the building. We would like to say a very big thank you to all of those people involved with the **Olivier Appeal** particularly the **Theatres' Restoration Fund**, the **Rayne Foundation**, the **Foundation for Sport and the Arts** and the **Arts Council's Incentive Funding Scheme** and hope that they continue to support us in this new and exciting phase in the Royal Court's history, as we complete the refurbishment with the new **Arts Council** funding.

As Stephen Daldry, Artistic Director states: *'The Theatre is in such a terrible physical state at the moment that without this funding we would not have been able to survive more than about 18 months. This would have meant the end of this unique and wonderful playhouse. Now we can face the future with confidence and carry on the work of promoting new plays and playwrights'*

Development plans include a complete renovation of the theatre - without losing any of its unique charm and relaxed atmosphere. Access will be improved, including facilities for wheelchairs. Theatre-goers will enjoy vastly better conditions including improved seating in the auditorium and larger and better equipped refreshment areas. Funds have also been provided for a feasibility study into a new performance space for the Royal Court Young People's Theatre enabling it to continue its important work.

The Royal Court still faces a huge task to raise the additional partnership funding of £5 million necessary to secure the **Arts Council** funding. With your help we are confident of meeting our target. A tour of the theatre, including its more picturesque parts, can be arranged by ringing **Josephine Campbell on 0171 730 5174**. If you would like to help with an event or gift please ring **Jacqueline Simons, Development Manager on 0171 823 4132**.

'Secure the theatre's future, and take it forward towards the new century. For the health of the whole theatrical life of Britain it is essential that this greatly all providing theatre we love so much and wish so well continues to prosper.'
Laurence Olivier *1988*

The English Stage Company at the Royal Court Theatre

The English Stage Company was formed to bring serious writing back to the stage. The Court's first Artistic Director, George Devine, wanted to create a vital and popular theatre. He encouraged new writing that explored subjects drawn from contemporary life as well as pursuing European plays and forgotten classics. When John Osborne's *Look Back in Anger* was first produced in 1956, it forced British Theatre into the modern age. But, the Court was much more than a home for 'Angry Young Men' illustrated by a repertoire that stretched from Brecht to Ionesco, by way of J P Sartre, Marguerite Duras, Wedekind and Beckett.

The ambition to discover new work which was challenging, innovative and also of the highest quality became the fulcrum of the Company's work. Early Court writers included Arnold Wesker, John Arden, David Storey, Ann Jellicoe, N F Simpson and Edward Bond. They were followed by a generation of writers led by David Hare and Howard Brenton, and in more recent years, celebrated house writers have included Caryl Churchill, Timberlake Wertenbaker, Robert Holman and Jim Cartwright. Many of their plays are now regarded as modern classics.

Since 1994 the Theatre Upstairs has programmed a major season of plays by writers new to the Royal Court, many of them first plays, produced in association with the **Royal National Theatre Studio** with sponsorship from **The Jerwood Foundation**. The writers include Joe Penhall, Nick Grosso, Judy Upton, Sarah Kane, Michael Wynne, Judith Johnson, James Stock and Simon Block.

Many established playwrights had their early plays produced in the Theatre Upstairs including Anne Devlin, Andrea Dunbar, Sarah Daniels, Jim Cartwright, Clare McIntyre, Winsome Pinnock, and more recently Martin Crimp and Phyllis Nagy.

Theatre Upstairs productions have regularly transferred to the Theatre Downstairs, as with Ariel Dorfman's *Death and the Maiden*, and this autumn Sebastian Barry's *The Steward of Christendom*, a co-production with Out of Joint.

1992-1995 were record-breaking years at the box-office with capacity houses for productions of *Faith Healer*, *Death and the Maiden*, *Six Degrees of Separation*, *King Lear*, *Oleanna*, *Hysteria*, *Cavalcaders*, *The Kitchen*, *The Queen & I*, *The Libertine*, *Simpatico*, *Mojo* and *The Steward of Christendom*.

Death and the Maiden and *Six Degrees of Separation* won the Olivier Award for Best Play in 1992 and 1993 respectively. *Hysteria* won 1994's Olivier Award for Best Comedy, and also the Writers' Guild Award for Best West End Play. *My Night with Reg* won the 1994 Writers' Guild Award for Best Fringe Play, the Evening Standard Award for Best Comedy, and Best Comedy in this year's Olivier Awards. Jonathan Harvey won the 1994 Evening Standard Drama Award for Most Promising Playwright, for *Babies*. Sebastian Barry won the 1995 Writers' Guild Award for Best Fringe Play for *The Steward of Christendom*, Jez Butterworth was named New Writer of the Year for *Mojo* by the Writers' Guild, and also won the Evening Standard Award for Most Promising Newcomer 1995. Phyllis Nagy won the Writers' Guild Award for Best Regional Play for *Disappeared*. The Royal Court has just been awarded the 1995 Prudential Award for the Arts (theatre) for creativity, excellence, innovation and accessibility, and the 1995 Peter Brook Empty Space Award for innovation and excellence in theatre.

After nearly four decades, the Royal Court's aims remain consistent with those established by George Devine. The Royal Court Theatre is still a major focus in the country for the production of new work. Scores of plays first seen in Sloane Square are now part of the national and international dramatic repertoire.

The Changing Room

To Jake

Characters

Harry	Cleaner: 50–60
Patsy	Wing threequarter: 23–5
Fielding	Forward: 35–6
Mic Morley	Forward: 28
Kendal	Forward: 29
Luke	Masseur: 40–50
Fenchurch	Wing threequarter: 23–5
Colin Jagger	Centre threequarter: 26
Trevor	Full-back: 26
Walsh	Forward: 35–40
Sandford	Assistant trainer: 40
Barry Copley	Scrum-half: 27–8
Jack Stringer	Centre threequarter: 30
Bryan Atkinson	Forward: 32
Billy Spencer	Reserve: 20
John Clegg	Hooker: 30
Frank Moore	Reserve: 21
Danny Crosby	Trainer: 45–50
Cliff Owens	Stand-off half: 30–32
Tallon	Referee
Thornton	Chairman: 50
Mackendrick	Club Secretary: 60

The Changing Room was first presented at the Royal Court Theatre, London, on November 9th, 1971, with the following cast:

Harry	John Barrett
Patsy	Jim Norton
Fielding	David Daker
Mic Morley	Edward Peel
Kendal	Warren Clarke
Luke	Don McKillop
Fenchurch	Peter Childs
Colin Jagger	Mark McManus
Trevor	Michael Elphick
Walsh	Edward Judd
Sandford	Brian Glover
Barry Copley	Geoffrey Hinsliff
Jack Stringer	David Hill
Bryan Atkinson	Peter Schofield
Billy Spencer	Alun Armstrong
John Clegg	Matthew Guinness
Frank Moore	John Price
Danny Crosby	Barry Keegan
Cliff Owens	Frank Mills
Tallon	Brian Lawson
Thornton	Paul Dawkins
Mackendrick	John Rae

Directed by Lindsay Anderson
Designed by Jocelyn Herbert

Act One

A changing room; afternoon. The light comes from glazed panels high in the wall and from an electric light.

Across the back of the stage is the main changing bench, set up against the wall and running its entire length. A set of hooks, one for each player, is fastened at head height to the wall, with the name of a player above each hook. Underneath the bench, below each hook, is a locker, also labelled. A jersey and a pair of shorts have been set out beneath one of the hooks. A rubbing-down table with an adjustable head-rest stands in front of the bench. Stage right, a glazed door opens to an entrance porch. Downstage left is a fireplace, with a bucket of coal, overhung by a mirror advertising ale. Upstage left is the open entry to the bath and showers: buckets, stool, hose and tap, etc. Downstage right is a wooden door, closed, leading to the offices. A second table stands against the wall. There's a pair of metal scales with individual metal weights on a metal arm. By the rubbing-down table stands a large wickerwork basket. A wooden chair with a rounded back is set against the wall, stage left.

Tannoy music is being played, light, militaristic.

Harry *enters from the bath. He's a broken-down man, small, stooped, in shirt-sleeves, rolled, and a sleeveless pullover. He's smoking and carries a sweeping-brush, on the lookout for anything he might have missed. He sweeps, looks round the floor, sweeps; finally lifts corner of the boxed-in rubbing-down table and sweeps the debris underneath. Takes out his cigarette, looks round, finds nowhere to drop it, then crosses to the fire; drops it in, sets the brush against the wall, puts coal from the bucket on the fire, warms his hands, shivers.*

Patsy *enters from the porch. He's a smart, lightly built man, very well groomed, hair greased, collar of an expensive overcoat turned up. Brisk, businesslike, narcissistic, no evident sense of humour.*

Patsy Harry . . .

Harry Patsy . . .

Patsy Cold.

Harry   Bloody freezing, lad. (*Rubs his hands; reaches to the fire again.*)

Patsy, *evidently familiar with his routine, goes to his locker. Gets out his boots, unfolds his jersey and shorts already lying on the bench.*

Patsy   No towel.

Harry   No. No. Just fetching those . . . (*Takes his brush and exits through bath entrance.*)

Patsy, *having checked his jersey, examined its number (2), collar, etc. – no marks – does the same with his boots: laces, studs, lining. He then crosses to the fire, takes out a comb from an inside pocket and smooths his hair down in the mirror. He's doing this as* **Harry** *re-enters carrying several neatly folded towels. He puts one on the bench by* **Patsy**'s *peg, then goes to the wickerwork basket, lifts the lid and gets out several more towels. Having checked them, counting soundlessly to himself, he puts them all in the basket, save three which he begins to arrange on the massage table.*

Patsy, *having combed his hair and admired himself in the mirror, clears his nose and spits in the fire.*

Harry   (*laying out towels*)   Thought it'd be snowed off.

Patsy   Snow?

Harry   Bloody forecast.

Patsy   Not cancel ought in this dump, I can tell you . . . Shoulder . . . I've no skin on from here to here. There's not a blade o' grass on that bloody pitch . . . sithee . . . look at that . . .

Pulls up his sleeve. **Harry** *looks across with no evident interest.*

Harry   Aye.

Patsy   Watered t'bloody pitch we 'ad last week. Froze over ten minutes after. Took a run at t'bloody ball . . . took off . . . must have travelled twenty bloody yards without having lift a finger.

Harry   Aye.

Patsy   Ice.

Harry *is laying out the rest of the jerseys now, and shorts.*

Patsy   Be better off with a pair of skates. (*Glances behind him, into the mirror; smooths hair.*) If there's a young woman comes asking for me afterwards, will you tell her to wait up in the office? Be frozen to death out theer.

Harry   Aye . . .

Patsy   By Christ . . . (*Rubs his hands, standing with his back to the fire.*)

Harry   Comes from Russia.

Patsy   What?

Harry   Cold . . . Comes fro' Russia . . .

Patsy   Oh . . . (*Nods.*)

Harry   Read a book . . . they had a special machine . . . blew these winds o'er, you see . . . specially freezing . . . mixed it with a chemical . . . frozen ought . . . Froze the entire country . . . Then Ireland . . . Then crossed over to America and froze it out . . . Then, when everything wa' frozen, they came o'er in special boots and took over . . . Here . . . America . . . Nobody twigged it. Nobody cottoned on, you see.

Patsy   Oh . . . (*Glances at himself in mirror again.*) You think that's what's happening now, then?

Harry   Cold enough . . . Get no warning . . . Afore you know what's happening . . . Ruskies here.

Patsy   Couldn't be worse than this lot.

Harry   What?

Patsy   Stopped ten quid i' bloody tax last week . . . I tell you . . . I'm paying t'government to keep me i' bloody work . . . madhouse . . . If I had my time o'er again I'd emigrate . . . America . . . Australia . . .

Harry   Wherever you go they'll find you out.

Patsy   What?

Harry   Ruskies . . . Keep your name down in a bloody book . . . (*Looks across.*) Won't make any difference if you've voted socialist. Have you down theer . . . up against a wall . . .

Patsy   Thy wants to read one or two bloody facts, old lad.

Harry   Facts? What facts? . . . I read in one paper that in twenty-five years not one country on earth'll not be communist . . .

Patsy *crosses back to his peg and starts taking off his overcoat.*

Don't worry. There'll be no lakin' bloody football then.

Patsy   They lake football i' Russia as much as they lake it here.

Harry   Aye . . .

Harry *waits, threatening;* **Patsy** *doesn't answer, preoccupied with his overcoat.*

You: football . . . You: coalmine . . . You: factory . . . You: air force . . . You . . . *Siberia.*

Patsy   Haven't you got a bloody coathanger? Damn well ask for one each week.

Harry   Aye. Don't worry . . . (*Starts to go.*) Not bloody listen until they find it's bloody well too late. (*Goes off to the bath entrance, disgruntled.*)

Fielding *enters: large, well-built man, slow, easy-going, thirty-five to thirty-six. He's dressed in an overcoat and muffler; he has a strip of plaster above his left eye.*

Fielding   Patsy.

Patsy   Fieldy . . .

Fielding   Freeze your knuckles off today. (*Blows in hands, goes over to fire; stoops, warms hands.*) By Christ . . .

Patsy *is holding up his coat in one hand, dusting it down lightly, paying no attention to* **Fielding**'s *entrance.*

Harry *comes back in with wooden coathanger.*

Harry   Have no bloody servants theer, you know.

Patsy (*examining coat*)   What's that?

Harry   No servants. Do your own bloody carrying theer.

Gives **Patsy** *the hanger and goes back to laying out the playing-kit.*

Fielding   What's that, Harry? (*Winks to* **Patsy**.)

Patsy   Bloody Russians. Going to be invaded.

Harry   Don't you worry. It can happen any time, you know.

Patsy   Going to freeze us, with a special liquid . . . Then come over . . . (*To* **Harry**.) What wa're it? . . . i' special boots.

Harry   It all goes back, you know.

Patsy   Back?

Harry   To bloody Moscow . . . Ought you say here's reported back . . . Keep all thy names in a special book.

Fielding   Keep thy name in a special bloody book . . . Riley . . . First name: Harry . . . Special qualifications: can talk out of the back of his bloody head.

Harry   Don't you worry.

Fielding   Nay, I'm not worried. They can come here any day of the bloody week for me. Sup of ale . . .

Patsy   Ten fags . . .

Fielding   That's all I need. (*Sneezes hugely. Shakes his head, gets out his handkerchief, blows his nose, lengthily and noisily.*) Come on, then, Harry . . . Switch it off.

After gazing at **Fielding**, *threatening,* **Harry** *turns off the Tannoy.*

I thought o' ringing up this morning . . . Looked out o' the bloody winder. Frost . . . (*Crosses over to* **Patsy**.) Got this

house, now, just outside the town . . . wife's idea, not mine
. . . bloody fields . . . hardly a bloody sign of human life . . .
cows . . . half a dozen sheep . . . goats . . .

Starts peeling the plaster from above his eye. **Patsy** *pays no attention,
arranging his coat on the hanger and picking off one or two bits.*

Middle of bloody nowhere . . . if I can't see a wall outside on
t'window I don't feel as though I'm living in a house . . .
How's it look?

Patsy (*glances up, briefly*)   All right.

Fielding   Bloody fist. Loose forra'd . . . Copped him one
afore the end. Had a leg like a bloody melon . . . (*Feeling the
cut.*) Get Lukey to put on a bit of grease . . . Should be all
right. How's your shoulder?

Patsy   All right. (*Eases it.*) Came in early. Get it strapped.
(*Indicates, however, that there's no one here.*)

Fielding   Where we lived afore, you know, everything you
could bloody want: pit, boozer, bloody dogs. As for now . . .
trees, hedges, miles o' bloody grass . . . (*Inspecting his kit which*
Harry *has now hung up.*) Weer's the jock-straps, Harry? . . . I
thought of ringing up and backing out. Flu . . . some such
like. (*Sneezes.*) By God . . . He'll have me lakin' here, will
Harry, wi' me bloody cobblers hanging out.

Morley *has now entered from the porch: thick-set, squat figure, dark-
haired. Wears a jacket, unbuttoned, with a sweater underneath; hard,
rough, uncomplicated figure.*

Nah, Morley, lad, then: how's thy keeping?

Morley   Shan't be a second . . . Just o'd on. (*Goes straight
over to the bath entrance, unbuttoning his flies.*)

He's followed in by **Kendal**: *tall, rather well-built, late twenties,
wearing an old overcoat with a scarf, and carrying a paper parcel. A
worn, somewhat faded man.*

Harry *has gone to the basket and is now getting out a pile of jock-
straps which he lays on the table.*

Kendal (*to* **Harry**)   Here . . . see about my boots? Bloody stud missing last Thursday . . . (*To* **Fielding**.) Supposed to check them every bloody week. Come up to training and nearly bust me bloody ankle. God Christ, they don't give a sod about bloody ought up here . . . Patsy . . .

Patsy   Kenny . . . (*Having hung up his coat, starts taking of his jacket.*)

Kendal (*to* **Fielding**)   Bought one of these electric tool-sets . . .

Fielding (*to* **Patsy**)   Tool-sets . . .

Patsy *nods.*

Fielding   Got all the tools that I need, Kenny.

Kendal   Bloody saw . . . drill, bloody polisher. Just look.

Fielding   What do you do with that? (*Picks out a tool.*)

Kendal   Dunno.

Patsy   Takes stones out of hosses' hoofs, more like.

They laugh.

Morley *comes back in.*

Fielding   Dirty bugger. Pisses i' the bloody bath.

Morley   Been in that bog, then, have you? (*To* **Harry**.) You want to clean it out.

Harry   That lavatory was new this season . . . (*Indicating* **Fielding**.) He'll tell you. One we had afore I wouldn't have used.

Morley *goes straight to the business of getting changed: coat off, sweater, then shoes and socks; then starts examining his ankle.*

Fielding   Harry doesn't use a lavatory, do you?

Morley   Piles it up behind the bloody posts.

Fielding   Dirty bugger.

Harry   Don't worry. It all goes down.

Morley   Goes down?

They laugh.

Goes down where, then, lad?

Patsy   He's reporting it back, tha knows, to Moscow.

Morley   Moscow? Moscow?

Harry   Somebody does, don't you bloody worry. Everything they hear.

Fielding   Nay, Harry, lad. Thy should have warned us. (*Puts his arm round* **Harry***'s shoulder.*)

Harry   Don't worry. You carry on. (*Breaks away from* **Fielding***'s embrace.*) You'll be laughing t'other side of your bloody face. (*Exits.*)

Fielding (*holding jersey up*)   Given me number four, an' all. I'll be all right jumping up and down i' middle o' yon bloody backs.

Kendal   By God. (*Rubbing his hands at the fire.*) I wouldn't mind being on the bloody bench today.

Pause. **Luke** *comes in, wearing a track-suit and baseball shoes and carrying a large hold-all, plus a large tin of Vaseline; sets them down by the massage table. A small, middle-aged man, perky, brisk, grey-haired.*

Fielding   Nah, Lukey, lad. Got a drop o' rum in theer, then, have you?

Luke   Aye. Could do with it today.

Morley   Lukey . . .

Kendal   Lukey . . .

Luke   Who's first on, then? (*Indicating the table.*) By Christ . . . (*Rubs his hands.*)

Patsy   My bloody shoulder . . .

Luke   Aye. Right, then. Let's have a look. (*Rummaging in his bag; gets out crêpe bandage.*)

Patsy *is stripped to his shirt by now; takes it off, hangs it and comes over in his vest and trousers. Sits on the edge of table for* **Luke** *to strap him up.*

Morley   Bloody ankle, Lukey . . .

Luke   Aye. All right.

Fielding (*examining* **Patsy**'*s shoulder*)   By God, there's nowt theer, lad. Which shoulder wa're it?

Morley   Sprained it.

Fielding   Sprained it.

Morley   Twisted it i' bed.

They laugh. **Patsy** *pays no attention. Holds his elbow as if one shoulder gives him great pain.*

Harry *comes back in with remaining jerseys.*

Luke   Right, then, lad. Let's have it off.

Having got out all his equipment, **Luke** *helps* **Patsy** *off with his vest.*

Kendal (*to* **Morley**)   Look at that, then, eh? (*Shows him his tool-kit.*) Sand-paper . . . polisher . . . circular saw . . .

Fielding (*stripping*)   What're you going to mek with that, then, Kenny?

Kendal   Dunno . . . shelves.

Morley   What for?

Kendal   Books.

Fielding (*laughs*)   Thy's never read a bleeding book.

Kendal   The wife reads . . . Got three or four at home.

Morley *laughs.*

Cupboards . . . Any amount o' things . . . Pantry door. Fitments . . .

Fielding   Fitments.

They laugh: look over at **Kendal***; he re-examines the tools inside the parcel.*

Morley   T'only bloody fitment thy needs, Kenny . . . Nay, lad, they weern't find wrapped up inside that box.

They laugh; **Fielding** *sneezes.* **Kendal** *begins to pack up his parcel.* **Harry** *has gone out, having set the remaining jerseys. The door from the porch opens:* **Fenchurch, Jagger** *and* **Trevor** *come in.*

Fenchurch *is a neatly groomed man, small, almost dainty; wears a suit beneath a belted raincoat. He carries a small hold-all in which he keeps his boots: self-contained, perhaps even at times a vicious man.*

Jagger *is of medium height, but sturdy. He wears an overcoat, with an upturned collar, and carries a newspaper: perky, rather officious, cocky.*

Trevor *is a studious-looking man; wears glasses, is fairly sturdily built. Quiet, level-headed: a schoolmaster.*

Fielding   Fenny.

Morley   Fenchurch.

Fenchurch   Na, lad.

Jagger   Come up in old Fenny's bloody car . . . (*To* **Luke.**) By God: nearly needed thee there, Lukey . . . Blind as a bloody bat is yon . . . Old feller crossing the bleedin' road: tips him up the arse with his bloody bumper.

Fenchurch   He started coming backwards. In't that right, then, Trevor?

Trevor   Aye. He seemed to.

Luke   Did he get your name?

Jagger   Old Fenny gets out of the bleedin' car . . . How much did you give him?

Fenchurch   A bloody fiver.

Trevor   A ten-bob note.

Jagger   The bloody miser . . .

Trevor   Bends down, tha knows . . .

Jagger   He picks him up . . .

Trevor   Dusts down his coat . . .

Jagger   Asks him how he was . . . Is that right? That's all you gave him?

Fenchurch   Gone to his bloody head if I'd have given him any more.

They laugh.

Trevor (*instructional*)   You told him who you were, though, Fen.

Jagger   Offered him his bloody autograph.

They laugh.

Morley   I went up to Fenny's one bloody night . . . He said, 'I won't give you my address . . . just mention my name to anyone you see . . . ' Stopped a bobby at the end of his bloody road: 'Could you tell me where Gordon Fenchurch lives? Plays on the wing for the bloody City?' 'Who?' he said. '*Who?*' 'Fenchurch.' 'Fenchurch? Never heard of him.'

They laugh. **Fenchurch**, *taking no notice of this, has merely got out his boots and begun to examine them.*

Harry *has come in with boots.*

Jagger   Ay up, ay up. Ay up. He's here. Look what the bloody ragman's brought.

Walsh *comes in: a large, somewhat commanding figure. He wears a dark suit with a large carnation in the buttonhole. He enters from the offices, pausing in the door. He's smoking a cigar. His age, thirty-five to forty. Stout, fairly weatherbeaten. There are cries and mocking shouts at his appearance: 'Ay up, ay up, Walshy, then.' 'What's this?'*

Walsh   And er . . . who are all these bloody layabouts in here?

Fielding   The bloody workers, lad. Don't you worry.

Walsh   I hope the floor's been swept then, Harry . . . Keep them bloody microbes off my chair . . . (*Comes in.*) Toecaps polished with *equal* brightness, Harry . . . (*To* **Jagger**.) I hate to find one toecap brighter than the next.

Jagger   White laces.

Walsh   White laces.

Harry *has set the boots down. Goes out.*

Morley   Where you been, then, Walshy?

Walsh   Been?

Fielding   Been up in the bloody offices, have you? (*Gestures overhead.*)

Walsh   . . . Popped up. Saw the managing director. Inquired about the pitch . . . Asked him if they could *heat it up* . . . thaw out one or two little bumps I noticed. Sir Frederick's going round now with a box of matches . . . applying a drop of heat in all the appropriate places . . . Should be nice and soft by the time you run out theer.

Fielding   Thy's not coming with us, then?

Walsh   Nay, not for bloody me to tell . . .

Morley   It's up to more important folk than Walsh . . .

Walsh   Not more important . . . more influential . . . (*Watching* **Trevor**.) Saw you last week with one of your classes, Trev . . . Where wa're it, now, then. Let me think . . .

Trevor   Don't know.

Walsh   Quite close to the Municipal Park . . . (*Winks to* **Jagger**.) By God, some of the girls in that bloody school . . . how old are they, Trev?

Trevor   Fourteen.

Walsh   Fourteen. Could have fooled me, old lad. Could have bloody well fooled me entirely. Old Trevor: guides them over the road, you know . . . *by hand.*

Fenchurch   Where have you been, then, Walshy?

Walsh (*conscious of his carnation quite suddenly, then cigar*) Wedding.

Jagger A wedding.

Walsh Not mine . . . Sister-in-law's as a matter of fact.

Trevor Sister-in-law?

Walsh Married to me brother. Just got married a second time. Poor lass . . . Had to come away. Just got going . . . T'other bloody team's arrived . . .

Jagger Seen the bus? (*Gestures size, etc.*)

Walsh Ran over me bloody foot as near as not . . . 'Be thy bloody head next, Walsh' . . . Said it from the bloody window! . . . Said, 'Bloody well get out theer and tell me then' . . . gesturing at the field behind.

They laugh.

Load o' bloody pansies. Tell it at a glance . . . Off back theer, as a matter of fact. Going to give a dance . . . Thy's invited, Jagger, lad. Kitted out . . . Anybody else fancy a dance tonight? Champagne . . . (*Belches: holds stomach.*) I'll be bloody ill if I drink owt else . . .

Luke Thy doesn't want to let old Sandford hear you.

Walsh Sandford. Sandford . . . Drop me from this team, old lad . . . I'd gi'e him half o' what I earned.

Luke One week's dropped wages and he's round here in a bloody flash.

Walsh There was some skirt at the bloody wedding, Jagger . . . (*To* **Trevor**.) Steam thy bloody glasses up, old lad.

Jagger You're forgetting now . . . Trevor here's already married.

Walsh She coming to watch, then, Trev, old lad?

Trevor Don't think so. No.

Walsh   Never comes to watch. His wife . . . A university degree . . . what wa're it in?

Trevor   Economics.

Walsh   Economics . . . (*To* **Fenchurch**.) How do you fancy being wed to that?

Fenchurch *goes off through bath entrance.*

Jagger   Wouldn't mind being married to bloody ought, wouldn't Fenny.

Fielding   Tarts: should see the bloody ones he has.

Walsh *has warmed his hands, rubbing.*

Walsh   Kenny: how's thy wife keeping, then, old lad?

Kendal   All right.

Walsh (*looking in the parcel*)   Bought her a do-it-yourself kit, have you?

Kendal   Bought it for meself.

Morley   Going to put up one or two shelves and cupboards . . . and what was that, now?

Fielding   Fitments.

Morley   Fitments.

Walsh   By Christ, you want to be careful theer, old lad . . . Ask old Jaggers. He's very keen on fitments.

Luke   Come on, Walsh. You'll be bloody well still talking theer when it's time to be going out . . . Morley: let's have a bloody look, old lad.

Harry *has come in with last boots.*

Luke *has strapped up* **Patsy**'s *shoulder.* **Patsy** *goes back to finish changing, easing his shoulder.*

Morley *comes over to the bench: sits down on it, half-lying, his legs stretched out.* **Luke** *examines his ankle: massages with oil; starts to strap it.*

Walsh *boxes with* **Jagger**, *then goes over to his peg.*

Walsh Sithee, Harry: I hope thy's warmed up Patsy's jersey.

Morley Don't want him catching any colds outside . . .

They laugh. **Patsy** *has taken his jersey over to the fire to warm, holding it in front of him.*

Fenchurch (*returning*) Seen that bloody bog?

Jagger Won't catch Sir Frederick, now, in theer.

Fenchurch Thy wants to get it seen to, Harry.

Harry Has been seen to . . .

Walsh Alus go afore I come. Drop off at the bloody peek-a-boo . . . now what's it called?

Jagger Nude-arama.

Walsh Best pair o' bogs this side o' town . . . Lukey, gi'e us a rub, will you, when I'm ready?

Slaps **Luke**'s *shoulder then backs up to the fire, elbowing* **Patsy** *aside.*

Luke *is strapping* **Morley**'s *ankle.*

Morley God Christ . . . go bloody steady. (*Winces.*)

Luke Does it hurt?

Morley Too tight.

Trevor (*watching*) Don't worry. It'll slacken off.

Harry *goes off.*

Fielding (*calling*)   What've you got on this afternoon, then, Jagger?

Jagger (*looking at his paper*)   A fiver.

Fielding   What's that, then?

Jagger   Two-thirty.

Walsh   Bloody Albatross.

Jagger   You what?

Walsh   Seven to one.

Jagger   You've never.

Walsh   What you got, then?

Jagger   Little Nell.

Harry *has come in with shoulder-pads and tie-ups.*

Walsh   Little Nell. Tripped over its bloody nose-bag . . . now, when wa're it . . .

Jagger   See thy hosses home, old lad.

Walsh   About ten hours after the bloody start.

They laugh.

Harry *is taking shoulder-pads to* **Jagger, Patsy, Fenchurch,** *dropping the tie-ups for the stockings on the floor, then taking the last of the shoulder-pads to Stringer's peg.* **Sandford** *has come in through the office door. He's a man of about forty, medium build; he wears an overcoat, which is now open, and carries a programme with one or two papers clipped to a pen. Stands for a moment in the door, sniffing. The others notice him but make no comment, almost as if he wasn't there.*

Sandford   I can smell cigar smoke . . . (*Looks round.*) Has somebody been smoking bloody cigars?

Walsh, *back to the fire, is holding his behind him.*

Jagger   It's Harry, Mr Sandford. He's got one here.

Walsh   That's not a bloody cigar he's got, old lad.

Harry   I don't smoke. It's not me. Don't worry.

They laugh.

Morley   Come on, now, Harry. What's thy bloody got?

Harry *avoids them as* **Jagger** *sets at him. Goes.*

Sandford (*to* **Walsh**)   Is it you, Ken?

Walsh   Me?

Fielding   Come on, now, bloody Walsh. Own up.

Walsh   Wheer would I get a bloody cigar? (*Puts the cigar in his mouth; approaches* **Sandford**.) I was bloody well stopped five quid this week. Thy never tossed me . . . What's it for, then, Sandy?

Sandford   Bloody language.

Walsh   Language?

Sandford   Referee's report . . . Thy wants to take that out.

Walsh   Out? (*Puffs.*)

Sandford *removes it; carefully stubs it out.*

Standford   You can have it back when you're bloody well dressed and ready to go home . . . If you want the report you can read it in the office.

Walsh   Trevor: exert thy bloody authority, lad. Players' representative. Get up in that office . . . (*To* **Sandford**.) If there's any been bloody well smoked I shall bloody well charge thee: don't thee bloody worry . . . Here, now: let's have it bloody back.

Takes it out of **Sandford**'s *pocket, takes* **Sandford**'s *pencil, marks the cigar.*

They laugh.

Warned you. Comes bloody expensive, lad, does that.

Puts cigar back. Goes over to bench to change.

Sandford (*to* **Morley**)   How's thy ankle?

Morley   All right. Bit stiff.

Luke (*to* **Sandford**)   It'll ease up. Don't worry.

Sandford   Patsy: how's thy shoulder?

Patsy   All right. (*Eases it, winces.*) Strapped it up. (*He's now put on a pair of shoulder-pads and is getting ready to pull on his jersey.*)

The others are now in the early stages of getting changed, though **Walsh** *has made no progress and doesn't intend to, and* **Fenchurch** *and* **Jagger** *are reading the racing page of the paper, still dressed.*

Harry *has come in. Puts down more tie-ups; wanders round picking up pieces from the floor, trying to keep the room tidy. The door from the porch opens and* **Copley** *comes in, limping, barging against the door. He's followed in by* **Stringer**. **Copley** *is a stocky, muscular man; simple, good-humoured, straightforward.* **Stringer** *is tall and slim; aloof, with little interest in any of the others. He goes straight to his peg and checks his kit; nods briefly to the others as he crosses.* **Copley** *staggers to the fire.*

Copley   God . . . It's like a bloody ice-rink out theer . . . Christ . . . (*Pulls up his trouser-leg.*)

Sandford   Are you all right . . .

Copley   Just look at that.

Walsh   Blood. Mr Sandford . . . Mr Sandford. Blood.

Copley   You want to get some salt down, Harry . . . (*To* **Sandford**.) Thy'll have a bloody accident out theer afore tonight.

Luke *crosses over to have a look as well. He and* **Sandford** *gaze down at* **Copley**'s *knee.*

Jagger   You all right, then, Stringer?

Stringer   Aye.

Jagger   No cuts and bruises.

Stringer   No.

Morley   Get nowt out of Stringer. In't that right, then, Jack?

Stringer *doesn't answer.*

Luke   Well, I can't see a mark.

Copley   Could'a sworn it wa' bloody cut.

Walsh   Wants to cry off there, Mr Sandford. (*To* **Copley**.) Seen the bloody pitch thy has.

Copley   Piss off.

They laugh.

Sandford (*to* **Stringer**)   Jack, then. You all right?

Stringer   Aye.

Sandford   Who else is there?

Jagger   There's bloody Owens: saw him walking up.

Fenchurch   Stopped to give him a bloody lift.

Jagger   Said he was warming up.

Walsh   Warming up!

Blows raspberry. They laugh.

Jagger   Silly prick.

Sandford (*to* **Trevor**)   You all right?

Trevor   Thanks.

Sandford   Saw your wife the other night.

Trevor   So she said.

Walsh   Ay, ay. Ay, ay . . .

Fenchurch   Heard that.

Walsh   Bloody Sandford . . .

Jagger   Coach old Trevor, Sandy, not his wife.

Sandford   It was a meeting in the Town Hall, as a matter of fact.

Walsh   Sithee – Harry: pricked up his bloody ears at that.

Fielding   What was the meeting about, then, Mr Sandford?

Sandford   Just a meeting.

Fenchurch   Town Hall, now: that's a draughty bloody place, is that.

They laugh.

Harry *goes out.*

Walsh   Come on, now, Trevor. What's it all about?

Trevor   Better ask Mr Sandford.

Walsh   He'll have no idea. Can't spell his name for a bloody start.

They laugh.

The door opens: **Atkinson** *comes in, followed by* **Spencer, Clegg** *and* **Moore**.

Atkinson   Jesus! Jesus! Lads! Look out! (*Crosses, rubbing hands, to fire.*)

Clegg   How do. How do. (*Follows him over to the fire, rubbing hands.*) By God, but it's bloody freezing.

Atkinson *is a tall, big-boned man, erect, easy-going. He wears a threequarter-length jacket and flat cap.*

Clegg *is a square, stocky, fairly small man, bare-headed, in an overcoat and scarf.*

Morley   Here you are, then, Cleggy. I've gotten the spot just here, if you want to warm your hands.

They laugh.

Spencer *and* **Moore** *are much younger men. They come in, nervous, hands in pockets.*

How's young Billy keeping, then?

Spencer   All right.

Walsh   Been looking after him, have you, Frank?

Moore   Be keeping a bloody eye on thee, then, Walsh.

Fielding   Babes in the bloody wood, are yon.

Atkinson Here, then. I hear that the bloody game's been cancelled.

Fenchurch Cancelled?

Copley Cancelled?

Fenchurch Cancelled?

Morley Here, then, Bryan: who told you that?

Atkinson A little bird . . .

Clegg We were coming up . . .

Atkinson Came over . . .

Clegg Whispered in his ear . . .

Jagger Give over . . .

Fenchurch Piss off.

Copley Rotten bloody luck.

Atkinson *and* **Spencer** *laugh.*

Sit on their bloody backsides up yonder.

Morley Give ought, now, to have me hands in Sir Frederick's bloody pockets . . .

Walsh Dirty bloody sod . . .

Morley Warming. Warming . . .

Walsh Come on, now, Sandy. Let it out. (*To* **Atkinson** *and* **Clegg**.) He's been having it off here, now, with Trevor's wife.

Trevor All right, Walsh.

Luke We've had enough of that.

Sandford The meeting . . . was about . . . a municipal centre.

Jagger A municipal what?

Fenchurch Centre.

Clegg Centre.

Sandford There you are. I could have told you.

Walsh Sir Frederick bloody Thornton.

Jagger What?

Walsh Going to build it . . .

Sandford That's right.

Walsh Votes for it on the bloody council . . .

Jagger Puts in his tender . . .

Sandford He's not even on the council.

Clegg All his bloody mates are, though.

Sandford He asked me to attend, as a matter of fact. There are more important things in life than bloody football.

Clegg Not today there isn't.

Sandford Not today there, John, you're right . . . Now, then, Frank: are you all right?

Moore Aye.

Sandford Billy?

Spencer Aye. I'm fine.

Sandford Right. Let's have you bloody well stripped off . . . None of you seen Clifford Owens, have you?

Moore No.

Spencer No . . .

Sandford (*looking at watch*) By God: he's cutting it bloody fine.

With varying speeds, they've all started stripping off. **Harry** *has distributed all the kit and checked it.* **Luke**, *after strapping* **Morley**'s *ankle, has started strapping* **Stringer**'s *body, wrapping it round and round with tape,* **Stringer** *standing by the table, arms held out.*

Walsh (*to* **Sandford**) Here, then . . . Get a bit of stuff on . . . Let's see you do some bloody work.

Walsh *lies down on the table.*

Luke *has put his various medicine bottles from his bag by the table.*
Sandford *opens one, pours oil onto the palm of his hand and starts to rub* **Walsh** *down.*

Kendal   Is there anywhere I can keep this, Lukey?

Copley   What you got in there, Kenny?

Morley   He's bought an electric tool-kit, Luke.

Kendal   Aye.

Fielding   Show him it, Kenny. Let him have a look.

Kendal   Drill . . . electric polisher . . . sandpaper . . . electric saw . . . Do owt with that.

Shows it to **Copley**. **Fenchurch** *and* **Jagger** *look at it as well.*

Copley   We better tek it with us yonder, Kenny. Bloody well mek use o' that today.

They laugh.

Stringer   I've got one of those at home.

Kendal   Oh?

Stringer   Aye.

Jagger (*winking at the others*)   Is that right, then, Jack?

Stringer   Get through a lot o' work wi' that.

Jagger   Such as?

Kendal   Bookcases.

Jagger   Bookcases?

Stringer   I've made one or two toys, an' all.

Kendal   Any amount of things.

Stringer   That's right.

Fenchurch   Who did you give the toys to, Jack?

Stringer   What?

Jagger   Toys.

Stringer   Neighbour's lad . . .

Fenchurch   Your mother fancies you, then, with one of those?

Stringer   She doesn't mind.

Copley   You ought to get together here with Ken.

Atkinson   Bloody main stand could do with a few repairs.

They laugh.

Walsh   Take no bloody notice, Jack . . . If thy's got an electric tool-kit, keep it to thysen . . . Here, then, Sandy . . . lower . . . lower!

They laugh.

By God, I could do that better, I think, mesen.

Luke   Kenny: leave it with me, old lad. I'll keep an eye on it . . . Anybody else now? Fieldy: how's thy eye?

Fielding   Be all right. A spot of bloody grease.

Luke (*to* **Copley**)   Barry. Let's have your bloody back, old lad. (*Gets out more bandage.*)

Stringer *and* **Fenchurch** *have put on shoulder-pads.* **Patsy**, *changed and ready, crosses to the mirror to comb his hair and examine himself; gets out piece of gum, adjusts socks, etc.*

The tin of grease stands on the second table by the wall. After the players have stripped, got on their shorts, they dip in the tin and grease up: legs, arms, shoulders, neck, ears. The stockings they fasten with the tie-ups **Harry** *has dropped on the floor. A slight air of expectation has begun to filter through the room: players rubbing limbs, rubbing hands together, shaking fingers, flexing; tense.*

At this point **Crosby** *comes in. He's dressed in a track-suit and enters from the office. A stocky, gnarled figure, late forties or fifties.*

Crosby   Come on . . . come on . . . half ready . . . The other team are changed already . . .

Calls of 'Ah, give over', 'Get lost', 'Silly sods', etc.

Sandford   Clifford hasn't come yet, Danny.

Crosby   He's upstairs.

Walsh Upstairs?

Crosby (*looking round at the others, on tip-toe, checking those present*) Bill? Billy?

Spencer (*coming out*) Aye . . . I'm here.

Crosby Frank?

Moore Aye . . . I'm here.

Crosby On the bench today, then, lads.

Sandford *slaps* **Walsh** *who gets up to finish changing.* **Clegg** *lies down to be massaged.* **Luke** *is strapping* **Copley**'s *body with crêpe bandage and strips of plaster.*

Walsh What's old Owens doing upstairs?

Crosby Minding his own bloody business, lad.

Clegg Having a word with His Highness, is he?

Crosby Patsy. How's your shoulder, lad?

Patsy All right . . . stiff . . . (*Eases it up and down in illustration.*)

Crosby Fieldy. How's thy eye?

Fielding All right.

Crosby (*suddenly sniffing*) Bloody cigars. Who the hell's been smoking?

Luke What?

Crosby Not ten minutes afore a bloody match. Come on.

Sandford Oh . . . aye . . . here . . .

Crosby You know the bloody rule in here, then, Sandy?

Sandford Yes. Aye. Sorry. Put it out.

Luke Is Clifford changed, then, Danny?

Crosby (*distracted*) What?

Luke Need a rub, or strapping up, or ought?

Crosby Changed . . . He's gotten changed already.

Walsh Bloody well up theer? By God, then. Bridal bloody suite is that.

Crosby Jack? All right, then, are you?

Stringer Fine. Aye . . . Fine. All right.

Crosby Trevor?

Trevor All right.

Crosby Bloody well hard out theer. When you put 'em down . . . knock 'em bleeding hard.

Walsh And what's Owens bloody well been up to? Arranging a bloody transfer, is he? Or asking for a rise?

They laugh.

Crosby (*reading from a list*) Harrison's on the wing this afternoon, Patsy. Alus goes off his left foot, lad.

Patsy Aye. Right. (*Rubs arms, legs, etc.*)

He and **Clegg** *laugh.*

Crosby Scrum-half: new. Barry: when you catch him knock him bloody hard . . . Morley?

Morley Aye.

Crosby Same with you. Get round. Let him know you're theer . . . Same goes for you, Bryan.

Atkinson Aye.

Crosby Kenny . . . Let's see you bloody well go right across.

Morley He's brought something to show you here, Mr Crosby.

Crosby What?

Morley Kenny . . . Show him your bloody outfit, Ken.

Kendal (*after a certain hesitation*) Piss off!

They laugh.

Walsh You tell him, Kenny, lad. That's right.

Jagger (*to* **Kendal**) Anybody gets in thy road . . . (*Smacks his fist against his hand.*)

Clegg Ne'er know which is bloody harder. Ground out yon or Kenny's loaf.

They laugh.

Crosby Jack . . . Jagger . . .

Stringer Aye.

Jagger Aye . . .

Crosby Remember what we said. Keep together . . . don't be waiting theer for Trev . . . If Jack goes right, then you go with him . . . Trevor: have you heard that, lad?

Trevor Aye.

Crosby Use your bloody eyes . . . John?

Clegg Aye?

Crosby Let's have a bit of bloody service, lad.

Clegg Cliff been complaining, has he?

Crosby Complained about bloody nowt. It's me who's been complaining . . . Michaelmas bloody Morley . . . when you get that bloody ball . . . remember . . . don't toss it o'er your bloody head.

Walsh Who's refereeing then, old lad?

Crosby Tallon.

Groans and cries.

Jagger Brought his bloody white stick, then, has he?

Fenchurch Got his bloody guide-dog, then?

Crosby (*undisturbed; to* **Copley**) Watch your putting in near your own line, Barry . . . No fists. No bloody feet. Remember

. . . But when you hit them. Hit them bleeding hard. (*Looks at his watch.*) There's some gum. Walshy: how's thy back?

Walsh   She told me, Danny, she'd never seen ought like it.

They laugh.

Crosby *drops the packets of chewing-gum on the table. Goes over to talk to the players separately, helping them with jerseys, boots, etc.*

Clegg *gets up from the table.* **Jagger** *comes to have his leg massaged by* **Sandford.**

Faint military music can be heard from outside, and the low murmur of a crowd.

Fielding *comes over to have his eye examined by* **Luke**: *he greases it over.* **Fielding** *goes back.*

Crosby   Any valuables: let me have 'em . . . Any watches, ear-rings, anklets, cigarettes . . .

All   Give over. Not bloody likely. Safer to chuck 'em out o' bloody winder . . .

Laughter. **Crosby, Luke** *and* **Sandford** *take valuables and put them in their pockets.*

Owens *comes in through the office door, dressed in a track-suit: bright red with 'CITY' on the back; underneath he's already changed. Medium build, unassuming, bright, about thirty to thirty-two years old, he's rubbing his hands together, cheerful. A shy man, perhaps, but now a little perky.*

Owens   All right, then. Are we ready?

Jagger   Sod off.

Fenchurch   Give over.

Fielding   Where you been?

Cries and shouts.

Harry *has come in with track-suits; gives them to* **Moore** *to give out. Goes out.*

Owens Told me upstairs you were fit and ready. 'Just need you, Cliff,' they said, 'to lead them out.'

Walsh And how's Sir Frederick keeping, then?

Owens Asked me to come up a little early.

All Ay, ay. Ay, ay. What's that? Give over.

Owens Fill him in on the tactics we intend to use today.

Sandford That's right.

Jagger What tactics are those, then, Clifford?

Owens Told him one or two hand signals he might look out for, Jag.

They laugh.

The players are picking up gum, tense, flexing. Occasionally one or other goes out through the bath entrance, returning a few moments later.

Harry *has come in with buckets and bottles of water.*

Freeze the eyeballs off a copper monkey, boy, today. By God . . . (*Goes over to the fire.*) Could do with a bit more coal on, Harry.

Sandford You want to keep away from that bloody fire . . .

Luke Get cramp if you stand in front of that.

Walsh Got cramp in one place, Luke, already.

They laugh.

Owens Just watch the ball today, boy. Come floating over like a bloody bird.

Walsh If you listened to half he said afore a bloody match you'd never get out on that bloody field . . . Does it all, you

know, inside his bloody head . . . How many points do you
give us, then, today?

Owens   Sod all. You'll have to bloody earn 'em, lad.

Sandford   That's the bloody way to talk.

Crosby   Harry . . . where's the bloody resin board, old lad?

Jagger   Let's have a bloody ball, an' all.

Roar off of the crowd.

Harry *goes off through bath entrance.*

Morley   What bonus are we on today, then, Danny?

Crosby   All 'bonus thy'll get, lad, you'll find on t'end o' my
bloody boot . . . Now come on, come on, then, lads. Get
busy . . .

Crosby *is moving amongst the players; now all of them are almost
ready: moving over to the mirror, combing hair, straightening collars,
tightening boots, chewing, greasing ears, emptying coat pockets of
wallets, etc., and handing them to* **Crosby, Sandford** *or* **Luke.**

Tallon *comes in: a soldierly man of about forty, dressed in black
referee's shorts and shirt.*

Tallon   You all ready, then, in here?

Sandford   Aye. Come in, Mr Tallon. We're all ready, then.
All set.

Tallon   Good day for it.

Crosby   Aye. Take away a bit o' frost.

Tallon   Right. I'll have a look. Make sure that nobody's
harbouring any weapons.

A couple of players laugh.

Tallon *goes round to each player, examines his hands for rings, his
boots for protruding studs; feels their bodies for any belts, buckles or
protruding pads. He does it quickly; each player nods in greeting; one
or two remain aloof.*

As **Tallon** *goes round,* **Harry** *comes back with the resin board and two rugby balls; sets the board on the table against the wall. The players take the balls, feel them, pass them round, lightly, casual.*

Harry *moves off, to the bath entrance. He takes the coal-bucket with him.*

Owens *takes off his track-suit to several whistles; exchanges greetings, formally, with* **Tallon**.

After each player's been examined he goes over to the resin board, rubs his hands in the resin, tries the ball.

Spencer *and* **Moore** *have pulled on red track-suits over their playing-gear.*

Walsh   By God, I could do with wekening up . . . Lukey: where's thy bloody phials?

Owens   Off out tonight, then, Walshy, lad?

Walsh   I am. Two arms, two legs, one head. If you pass the bloody ball mek sure I'm bloody looking.

They laugh.

Owens   Ton o' rock there, Walshy, lad.

Walsh   Second bloody half . . . where wa're it? . . . 'Walshy! Walshy! Walshy!' . . . Passes . . . Fastening me bloody boot, what else.

Jagger   Never looks.

Walsh   Came down like a ton o' bloody lead.

They laugh.

Luke *has got out a tin of ammonia phials. The players take them, sniff, coughing, flinging back their heads; pass them on to the others. Several of the backs don't bother.* **Walsh** *takes his, breathes deeply up either nostril: no effect.*

Jagger   Shove a can o' coal-gas up theer: wouldn't make much bloody difference.

Walsh   Mr Tallon! Mr Tallon! You haven't inspected me, Mr Tallon!

They laugh. **Tallon** *comes over, finishing off.*

Tallon   All right, then, Walshy. Let's have a look.

Walsh, *arms raised, submits ponderously to* **Tallon**'s *inspection.*

Walsh   Count 'em! Count 'em! Don't just bloody look.

The players laugh.

Tallon *finishes, goes over to the door.*

Tallon (*to the room*)   Remember . . . keep it clean . . . play fair. Have a good game, lads. Play to the whistle.

All   Aye. All right.

Tallon   All right, then, lads. I'll see you. May the best team win. Good luck.

An electric bell rings as **Tallon** *goes out.*

Crosby   Okay. Five minutes . . . Forr'ads. Let's have you . . . Billy? Frank? You ready?

Moore   Aye.

Spencer   Aye . . .

Crosby   Over here, then. O'd these up.

Clegg *raises his arms;* **Walsh** *and* **Fielding** *lock in on either side, casual, not much effort.*

Atkinson *and* **Kendal** *bind together and put their heads in-between the three in front.*

Fielding   Ger off. Ger off!

Walsh   A bit lower there, then, Kenny . . . Lovely. Beautiful.

Clegg   Just right.

They laugh.

Crosby (*holding the forwards with* **Spencer** *and* **Moore**)   All right. All right.

Morley *leans on* **Atkinson** *and* **Kendal**, *then, at* **Crosby**'s *signal, puts his head between them as they scrum down.*

Spencer, Moore *and* **Crosby** *are linked together.*

Let's have a ball . . . Cliff . . . Barry . . . Number four: first clear scrum we get: either side . . . (*Takes the ball* **Sandford**'s *brought him.*) Our possession, theirs . . . Clifford . . . Jagger . . . Jack . . . that's right.

The rest of the players take up positions behind: **Copley** *immediately behind, then* **Owens**, *then* **Stringer, Jagger** *and* **Patsy** *on one side,* **Fenchurch** *on the other.* **Trevor** *stands at the back.*

Right, then? Our ball, then . . .

Crosby *puts the ball in at* **Clegg**'s *feet. It's knocked back through the scrum to* **Copley**; *then it's passed, hand to hand, slowly, almost formally, out to* **Patsy**. *As each player passes it, he falls back; the scrum breaks up, falls back to make a line going back diagonally and ending with* **Fenchurch**.

Walsh   From me. To you . . .

Laughter.

Crosby   All right. All right.

When the ball reaches **Patsy** *he passes it back: to* **Jagger**, *to* **Stringer**, *to* **Owens**, *to* **Copley**, *each calling the Christian name of the one who hands it on, until it reaches* **Fenchurch**.

Walsh   Run, Fenny! Run!

Jagger   Go on. Go on! It'll be t'on'y bloody chance thy has.

They laugh.

Walsh   I never know whether it's bloody speed or fear with Fenny . . . The sound of a pair of bloody feet behind.

Walsh *catches his backside. They laugh.*

Crosby   All right. All right . . . Trev: number six.

Sandford   Come up on your positions, lads: remember that.

They get down as before, though this time **Morley** *stands out and takes* **Copley**'s *place.* **Copley** *falls back;* **Owens** *falls back behind him.* **Jagger** *and* **Patsy** *stand on one side of* **Owens**, **Stringer** *and* **Fenchurch** *on the other;* **Trevor** *stands immediately behind him.*

Crosby   Remember: first time up . . . Cliff'll give his signal . . . our head; their put in . . . doesn't matter . . .

Crosby *puts the ball in the scrum as before. The forwards play it back between their feet.* **Morley** *takes it, turns, passes it back to* **Copley**; **Copley** *passes it back to* **Owens**, **Owens** *to* **Trevor**, *who runs and mimes a drop kick.*

Jagger   Pow!

Harry *has come in with coal-bucket.*

Walsh   Now thy's sure thy won't want thy glasses, Trev?

One or two laugh.

Trevor   Just about.

Walsh   If you can't see the posts just give a shout.

They laugh.

Jagger   Walshy here'll move 'em up.

Laughter.

Crosby   All right. All right. I'll say nowt else . . .

The door from the office has already opened.

Thornton *comes in: tall, dressed in a fur-collared overcoat. A well-preserved man of about fifty.*

He's accompanied by **Mackendrick**, *a flush-faced man of about sixty. He wears an overcoat, a scarf and a dark hat.*

Thornton   Hope I'm not intruding, Danny.

Crosby   No, no. Not at all.

Thornton   Thought I'd have a word.

Sandford   That's right.

Sandford *gestures at the players. They move round in a half-circle as* **Thornton** *crosses to the centre.*

Thornton   Chilly in here. That fire could do with a spot of stoking . . .

Mackendrick   Harry . . . spot o' coal on that.

Harry   Aye . . . Right . . . (*Mends the fire.*)

Thornton   Just to wish you good luck, lads.

Players   Thanks . . .

Thornton   Fair play, tha knows, has always had its just rewards.

Sandford   Aye . . .

Thornton   Go out . . . play like I know you can . . . there'll not be one man disappointed . . . Now, then. Any grunts and groans? Any complaints? No suggestions? (*Looks round.*)

Jagger   No . . .

Fenchurch   No, Sir Frederick . . .

Crosby   No.

Sandford   No, Sir Frederick . . .

Thornton   Right, then . . . Mr Mackendrick here'll be in his office, afterwards . . . if there's anything you want, just let him know . . . Good luck. Play fair. May the best team win . . . Cliff. Good luck.

Owens   Thanks. (*Shakes his hand.*)

Mackendrick   Good luck, Cliff . . . Good luck, lads . . .

Players   Aye . . . Thanks.

Thornton   Danny.

Crosby   Aye. Right . . . Thanks.

Thornton   Good luck, lads. See you later.

Mackendrick   Danny . . .

Thornton *waves, cheerily, and followed by* **Mackendrick**, *goes.*

Silence. Broken finally by **Harry**, *stoking fire.*

Crowd roars off; fanfare music; the opposing team runs on.

A bell rings in the room.

Crosby   Right, then, lads . . . Cliff? Ought you'd like to add?

Owens   No. (*Shakes his head.*) Play well, lads . . .

Players   Aye . . .

The players, tense, nervous, start to line up prior to going out.

Owens *takes the ball. He heads the column.*

Crowd roars again; loudspeaker, indecipherable, announces names.

Walsh   Harry: make sure that bloody bath is hot.

Harry *looks across. He nods his head.*

Towel out, tha knows . . . me bloody undies ready . . .

Crosby   Bloody Walsh . . . come on. Line up . . .

Groans, moans; the players line up behind **Owens (6)**.

> **Trevor (1)**
> **Patsy (2)**
> **Jagger (3)**
> **Stringer (4)**
> **Fenchurch (5)**
> **Copley (7)**
> **Walsh (8)**
> **Clegg (9)**
> **Fielding (10)**
> **Atkinson (11)**
> **Kendal (12)**
> **Morley (13)**

Spencer (15) *and* **Moore (14)**, *in red track-suits with 'CITY' on the back, are helping* **Luke** *and* **Sandford** *collect the various pieces of equipment: spare kit, track-suits, sponges, medical bag, spare ball, bucket.*

Crosby *holds the door.*

Owens   Right, then?

All   Right. Ready. Let's get off. (*Belches, groans.*)

Crosby   Good luck, Trev . . . good luck, lad . . . good luck . . . Good luck, Mic . . .

He pats each player's back as they move out. Moments after **Owens** *has gone there's a great roar outside.*

Crosby *sees the team out, then* **Spencer** *and* **Moore** *in track-suits, then* **Luke** *and* **Sandford**. *He looks round, then he goes, closing the door.*

The roar grows louder. Music.

Harry *comes in, wanders round, looks at the floor for anything that's been dropped, picks up odd tapes, phials. Goes to the fire; puts on another piece of coal, stands by it, still. The crowd roar grows louder.*

Then, slowly, lights and sound fade.

Act Two

The same. About thirty-five minutes later.

The dressing-room is empty, the light switched off. There's a faint glow from the fire.

The roar off of the crowd: rising to a crescendo, fading.

The door from the porch opens. **Thornton** *enters, rubbing his hands, followed by* **Mackendrick**.

Thornton By God . . . (*Gasps, shudders, stumbling round.*) Where's the light switch?

Mackendrick Here . . .

Light switched on.

Thornton How much longer?

Mackendrick (*looks at his watch*) Twelve . . . fifteen minutes.

Thornton Could do with some heating in that bloody box . . . either that or we watch it from the office. (*Crosses to the fire and warms his hands.*) Anybody in here, is there?

Mackendrick (*looks into the bath entrance*) Don't think so.

Thornton Got your flask?

Mackendrick Empty. (*Shows him.*)

Thornton (*rubbing his hands*) Send up to the office.

Mackendrick (*calls through the bath entrance*) Harry! (*Listens: no answer. Goes to office entrance.*)

Thornton You go, Mac . . . He'll be up in the bloody canteen, that lad. (*Has settled himself in the chair in front of the fire.*)

The crowd roars off.

Mackendrick Shan't be a second.

Thornton Second cabinet on the right: my office.

Mackendrick Right. (*Hesitates, goes off through office door.*)

Thornton *settles himself in front of the fire. Crowd roars off. He raises his head, listens.*

The roar dies. He leans forward, puts piece of coal on the fire.

Door bangs off; stamping of feet; coughs, growls, clearing of throat, sighs.

Harry *comes in from the bath entrance, muffled up: balaclava, scarf, cap, ex-army overcoat, gloves.*

Harry   Oh . . . Oh . . . (*On the way to the fire sees* **Thornton** *and stops, about to go back.*)

Thornton   That's all right. Come in, Harry . . . Taking a breather.

Harry   I just nipped up to the er . . .

Thornton   That's all right, lad.

Harry   Cup o' tea.

Thornton   Pull up a chair, lad. (*Moves his own over fractionally.*)

Harry *looks round. There's no other chair. He remains standing where he is.*

Nowt like a coal fire. Hardly get it anywhere now, you know . . . Synthetic bloody fuel. Like these plastic bloody chickens. Get nought that's bloody real no more.

Harry (*sways from one foot to the other*)   Aye . . .

Thornton   Water's hot, then, is it?

Harry   What?

Thornton   For the bath.

Harry   Oh. Aye . . . (*Pause.*) I've just stoked up.

Thornton   I'd have given you a hand myself if I'd have known. By God, that box . . . like ice . . . (*Takes hands out of his gloves.*) Can't feel a thing.

Harry   It comes fro' Russia.

Thornton   What?

Harry   The cold.

Thonton   Oh . . .

Harry   East wind . . . Blows from the Russian steppes.

Thornton (*looks up*)   More north-west today, I think.

Harry   Over the Baltic . . . Norway . . .

Thornton *has raised his hand. The crowd's roar rises; he listens.*
Harry *waits. The roar dies down.*

Thornton   Them, I think . . . Score today, our lads: they'll
raise the bloody roof.

Harry   I've read it in a book.

Thornton   What?

Harry   The Russians . . . when the wind blows to the west
– spray it with a special gas.

Thornton   Good God.

Harry   Without anybody knowing . . . Breathe it . . . Take
it in . . . (*Breathes in.*) Slows down your mind . . . (*Illustrates
with limp arms and hands.*) Stops everybody thinking.

Thornton   I think our lads've had a drop of that today. By
God, I've never seen so many bloody knock-ons . . . dropped
passes . . .

Harry   I've been a workman all my life.

Thornton   Oh . . . Aye.

Harry   I used to work in a brickyard afore I came up here.

Thornton   It's a pity you're not back theer, Harry lad.
Bloody bricks we get. Come to pieces in your bloody
hand . . . Had a house fall down the other day. Know what
it was . . . ? Bricks . . . crumbled up . . . Seen nothing like
it . . . Still . . .

Harry   Knew your place before. Now, there's everybody
doing summat . . . And nobody doing owt.

Thornton   Still. Go with it, Harry.

Harry   What . . .

Thornton   Can't go against your times . . . (*Twists round.*)
Sent Mac up for a bloody snifter . . . Had time to mek the
bloody stuff by now.

Crowd's roar rises; reaches crescendo; dies. Booing.

Don't know why they do that job, you know. Refereeing.
Must have a stunted mentality, in my view. To go on with a
thing like that.

Harry   Be all communist afore long.

Thornton   Aye. (*Pokes fire.*) If the Chinese don't get here
afore.

Harry   It's happening all the time. In the mind . . . Come
one day, they'll just walk in. Take over . . . There'll be
nobody strong enough to stop them. They'll have all been
brainwashed . . . You can see it happening . . .

Thornton (*calls*)   *Mac!* Takes that man a fortnight to brew a
cup of tea. Accountant . . . He'll be up there now, counting
the bloody gate receipts. I don't think he's at all interested in
bloody football . . . He's never slow, you know, to tell us
when we've made a bloody loss.

Banging outside. **Mackendrick** *comes in with the bottle.*

Thought you'd been swigging the bloody bottle.

Mackendrick   It wasn't in the cabinet . . . I had to get it
from the bar . . . Got to sign about four receipts . . .
Anybody gets a drink in this place they bloody well deserve
it, lad.

Thornton   No glasses?

Mackendrick   Here. (*Takes two from his pocket.*)

Thornton   Was that a score?

Mackendrick   Penalty. Missed.

Thornton   Them? Or us.

Mackendrick   Seven, two. Them. It'll take some pulling back . . . Harry. (*Nods.*)

Harry   Mr Mackendrick.

Mackendrick   Wrapped up for the weather, Harry.

Harry   Aye.

Thornton   Been telling me: comes from Russia.

Mackendrick   Russia.

Thornton   Weather.

Mackendrick   Weather!

Thornton   Might have bloody guessed . . . (*To* **Harry**.) Got a cup, then, have you? Try a drop o' this.

Harry   Don't drink. Thanks all the same, Sir Frederick.

Thornton   Nay, no bloody titles here, old lad. Freddy six days o' the week. (*To* **Mackendrick**.) Sir Frederick to the wife on Sundays.

Thornton *and* **Mackendrick** *laugh.*

Thornton *drinks.*

By God. Brings back a drop of life, does that.

Mackendrick   (*drinks, gasps*)   Grand . . . Lovely.

Roar of the crowd, huge, prolonged. They listen.

Thornton   Have a look. Go on. Quick. You've missed it . . .

Mackendrick *goes to the porch; disappears outside.*

How do you think they compare to the old days, Harry?

Harry   Players? . . . Couldn't hold a bloody candle . . . In them days they'd do a sixteen-hour shift, *then* come up and lake . . . Nowadays: it's all machines . . . and they're *still* bloody puffed when they come up o' Sat'days. Run round yon field a couple of times: finished. I've seen 'em laking afore with broken arms, legs broke . . . shoulders . . . Get a

scratch today and they're in here, flat on their bloody backs:
iodine, liniment, injections . . . If they ever played a real
team today they wouldn't last fifteen bloody seconds. That's
my view. That's what I think of them today. Everywheer.
There's not one of them could hold a candle to the past.

Roar and cheering from the crowd. **Thornton** *twists round and
listens.*

They'll wek up one morning and find it's all too late . . .

Mackendrick *comes back in.*

Mackendrick   Scored.

Thornton (*pleased*)   Try?

Mackendrick   Converted.

Thornton   Who wa're it?

Mackendrick   Morley.

Thornton   By God. Bloody genius that lad.

Mackendrick *pours a drink.*

Mackendrick   Harry . . . ?

Harry   No thanks, Mr Mackendrick.

Thornton   Harry here's been enlightening me about the
past . . . Nothing like the old days, Mac.

Harry   Aye!

Mackendrick   Bloody bunkum.

Thornton   What's that? (*Laughs: pleased.*)

Mackendrick   God Christ . . . If this place was like it was
twenty years ago – and that's not *too* far back – you wouldn't
find me here for a bloody start . . . As for fifty years ago.
Primeval . . . Surprised at thee, then, Harry lad.

Harry   Aye . . . (*Turns away.*)

Mackendrick   Have another snifter.

Thornton   Thanks.

Mackendrick *pours it in.*

Mackendrick (*to* **Harry**) I'd have thought thy'd see the difference, lad.

Harry *doesn't answer, turns away.*

Washed i' bloody buckets, then . . . et dripping instead o' bloody meat . . . urinated by an hedge . . . God Christ, bloody houses were nobbut size o' this – seven kiddies, no bloody bath: no bed . . . fa'ther out o' work as much as not.

Harry There's many as living like that right now!

Mackendrick Aye. And there's a damn sight more as not.

Thornton I never knew you had strong feelings, Mac.

Mackendrick About one or two bloody things I have.

He pours himself another drink. A faint roar from the crowd.

I suppose you're more on his side, then?

Thornton Nay, I'm on nobody's bloody side, old lad . . . I had a dream the other night . . . I was telling Cliff afore the match . . . I came up here to watch a match . . . looked over at the tunnel . . . know what I saw run out? (*Laughs.*) Bloody robots. (*Laughs again.*) And up in the bloody box were a couple of fellers, just like Danny, flicking bloody switches . . . twisting knobs. (*Laughs.*) I laugh now. I wok up in a bloody sweat, I tell you.

Roar from the crowd, applause.

Noises off: boots, shouting.

Ay up. Ay up . . . (*Springs up.*)

Harry You'll wake up one day . . . I've told you . . . You'll wek up one day . . . You'll find it's bloody well too late.

Goes off through bath entrance.

Mackendrick Aren't you staying to see them in?

Thornton I'll pop in in a couple of jiffies, lad . . . You stay and give 'em a bloody cheer . . . (*Slaps his shoulder.*) Shan't be long . . . (*Calls through to bath entrance.*) Harry . . . I'll pursue that argument another time. (*Nods, winks at* **Mackendrick,** *then goes out smartly through the office door.*)

Mackendrick *moves the chair from in front of the fire just as the players start to come in.*

Fenchurch *comes in first, shaking his hand violently. He's followed by* **Luke** *carrying his bag.*

Fenchurch Jesus! Jesus! Bloody hell.

Luke Here . . . Let's have a look. Come on.

Jagger (*following him in*) It's nothing . . . bloody nothing . . .

Fenchurch Bloody studs, you see . . . Just look!

He holds it up, wincing, as **Luke** *takes it. He groans, cries out, as* **Luke** *examines it.*

The others are beginning to flood in: stained jerseys, gasping, bruised, exhausted.

Harry *brings in two bottles of water; the players take swigs from them and spit out into* **Luke**'s *bucket which* **Moore** *has carried in.*

Luke Nothing broken. It'll be all right.

Sandford Do you want me to bind it for you, then?

Fenchurch No, no. No . . . No.

Jagger Can't hold the ball with a bandage on.

Copley Have you off to hospital, Fenny, lad. Match o'er: don't worry. Operation. Have it off. Not going to have you troubled, lad, by that.

Fenchurch Sod off.

They laugh.

Walsh, *groaning, collapses on the bench.*

Walsh I'm done. I'm finished. I shall never walk again. Sandy . . . Bring us a cup o' tea, old lad.

Sandford   You'll have a cup o' bloody nothing. Have a swab at that.

Splashes a cold sponge in **Walsh**'s *face and round his neck.* **Walsh** *splutters, groans; finally wipes his face and neck.* **Crosby** *has come in with the remainder of the players.*

Crosby   Well done. Well done. Start putting on the pressure in the second half.

Jagger   Pressure?

Fenchurch   Pressure . . .

Jagger   That *was* the bloody pressure. Anything from now on is strictly left-overs, Danny lad . . . I'm knackered. Look at that. Use hammers on that bloody pitch out theer . . .

Mackendrick   Well done, then, lads. Well done.

Fielding   You watching in here, then, Mr Mackendrick, are you?

Mackendrick   Out there, old lad. I wouldn't miss it.

Clegg   See that last try . . . ?

Mackendrick   . . . Go down in the bloody book will that.

Sandford   Keep moving. Don't sit still.

Crosby   That's right. Keep moving . . . Walshy. Get up off your arse.

Walsh *takes no notice, drinks from bottle.*

Bryan? How's your ankle?

Atkinson   All right. I think. It'll be all right.

Fielding   Just look at that. Can't move me bloody finger.

Crosby   Keep away from that bloody fire . . . Sandy: keep 'em moving round, old lad.

Luke *and* **Sandford** *are examining individual players.* **Moore** *and* **Spencer** *are helping out with laces, tightening boots, handing round the bottles.*

Any new jerseys? Any new shorts?

A couple of players call: 'No . . . No thanks.'

Copley   Over here, lads . . . I'll have one . . .

Crosby   Trevor? How's your hands?

Trevor   All right. (*Holds them up, freezing.*)

Crosby   Keep moving, lad. Keep shifting.

Trevor   Be all right. (*He is quite cold: hands and arms folded, then rubbing himself, trying to get warm.*)

Crosby   Barry?

Copley   No. No. All right.

Stringer   Bloody cold out theer. I read it i' the paper. Seven degrees of frost last night.

Sandford   Bloody well move faster, lad.

Stringer   I am moving faster. It bloody catches up with you.

Kendal   Ears, look. Can't bloody feel 'em.

Jagger   Still on, then, Kenny, are they?

Kendal   Aye. Think so. Better have a look. (*Crosses to mirror.*)

They're gradually getting over their first shock of entering the warmer room: sucking sponges, rinsing their mouths from the bottle, rubbing on more grease, adjusting boot-fastenings and socks. Those on the move move quite slowly, tired, panting.

Fenchurch   What's the bloody score, then, lads?

Fielding   Never notices on the bloody wing.

Copley   Picking his bloody nose.

Fielding   Talking to the crowd.

Moore   Seven–seven, Fenny, lad.

Clegg (*to* **Moore** *and* **Spencer**)   Bloody cold, you lads, out theer.

Spencer   Freezing.

Moore   Fro'zen.

Walsh   Mr Crosby, sir.

Crosby   What's that?

Walsh   Isn't it time we had a substitute out theer. These lads are dying to get on and lake.

Crosby   They'll get on in *my* bloody time, not yours. Now get up. Come on. Get moving. I've told thee, Walsh, before.

Patsy *is sitting down, having his leg 'stretched' by* **Sandford**: **Patsy**'s *leg stretched out before him,* **Sandford** *pressing back the toe of his boot.*

(*To* **Patsy**.) You all right?

Patsy   Bloody cramp. God . . . (*Groans, winces.*)

Walsh   Another bloody fairy . . .

Glegg   Go on. Give him summat, Sandy . . .

Walsh   Here. Let's have a bloody hold.

Patsy   S'all right. S'all right. S'all right. (*Springs up, flexes leg.*)

Walsh   S'all in the bloody mind, tha knows . . . Here. Have a look at my bloody back, then, will you?

Sandford *lifts his jersey at the back.*

Sandford   Got a cut.

Walsh   How many stitches?

Sandford   Twenty or thirty. Can't be sure.

Walsh   Go on. Go on. Get shut . . .

Players laugh.

Fieldy: have a bloody look, old lad.

Fielding *lifts* **Walsh**'s *shirt and looks; slaps* **Walsh**'s *back.*

Walsh *goes over to the bucket, gets sponge, squeezes it down his back.*

Luke (*calling, with liniment, etc.*)   Any more for any more?

Jagger   Any bruises, cuts, concussions, fractures . . .

Copley   One down here you could have a look at, Lukey.

Opens shorts: players laugh.

Thornton *has come in from the porch entrance.*

Thornton   Well played, lads. Well done . . . Morley: bloody fine try was that, young man.

Morley   Thank you, sir.

Thornton (*to* **Crosby**)   Not often we see a run like that . . .

Crosby   No. That's right.

Thornton   Good kick, Clifford. Good kick was that.

Owens   Aye. (*During this period he has been out, through the bath entrance, to wash his face and hands, almost like an office worker set for home. Has come in now, drying face and hands.*)

Thornton   Trevor: dropped goal: a bloody picture.

Trevor   Thanks.

Thornton   How're your hands?

Trevor   Frozen.

Thornton   Saw you catch that ball: didn't know you'd got it. (*Laughs.*)

Trevor   Numb . . . (*Laughs: rubs his hands.*)

Thornton   Kenny.

Kendal *nods.*

Walsh   Sir Frederick: how d'you think I managed, then?

Thornton   Like a dream, Walshy. Like a dream.

Jagger   Bloody nightmare, I should think, more likely.

The players laugh.

Crosby   He could bloody well do wi' wekening up . . .
There's half on you asleep out yon . . . Fieldy . . . Bryan . . .
move across. Go with it . . . It's no good waiting till they come
. . . Bloody hell . . . Trevor theer: he's covering all that side
. . . Colin: *bloody interceptions*: it's no good going in, lad, every
time . . . they'll be bloody well waiting for it soon . . . three
times that *I* saw, Jack here had to take your man . . .

Walsh   Billy?

Spencer   Aye?

Walsh   Go eavesdrop at their door, old lad.

Spencer   (*laughs*)   Aye!

Walsh   Find out all their plans.

They laugh.

Crosby   As for bloody Walsh. A boot up the backside
wouldn't go astray. I'll swear at times thy's running bloody
backwards, lad.

Walsh   I am. I bloody am . . . Too bloody cold today for
running forr'ad.

They laugh. **Walsh** *claps his cold hands either side of* **Sandford**'s
face. **Sandford**, *saying, 'Gerroff,' steps back.*

Crosby *goes into private, whispered conversation with individual
players.*

Mackendrick   How're you feeling, Trevor, lad?

Trevor   All right.

Mackendrick   Cut your ear there, lad . . . (*Examines it.*) Not
bad . . . Sandy? . . . Put a spot o' grease on that.

Sandford *comes across.* **Trevor** *winces.*

Take care of the professional men, you know. These lot –
(*Gestures round.*) bloody ten a penny.

Jeers. **Mackendrick** *takes no notice.*

Have you ever tried playing i' mittens, then?

Trevor   No.

Mackendrick Some players do, you know. Particularly in your position . . . In the amateur game, you know . . . Still. No need to tell you that, I'm sure.

Trevor Aye . . . I'll . . . just pop off in theer. Shan't be a minute.

Mackendrick Aye . . . aye! (*Slaps his back.*)

Trevor *goes off through bath entrance.*

Electric bell rings.

Crosby All right. All right. I'm saying no more. Quick score at the beginning: be all right . . . Cliff. At the fourth tackle, Cliff, try number five. (*To the rest.*) Have you got that?

Players Aye.

Crosby Be bloody ready . . . Patsy?

Patsy Aye.

Crosby Fenny?

Fenchurch Aye. All right.

Crosby Get *up* there! Bloody well stuck in.

Fenchurch Aye.

Crosby Bryan . . .

Atkinson Aye.

Crosby Harder. *Harder* . . . Kenny?

Kendal Aye?

Crosby *Bang 'em!* You're not tucking the buggers up in bed.

Kendal Aye.

Crosby Let's bloody well see it, then . . . I want to *hear* those sods go down . . . I want to feel that bloody stand start shaking . . . Johnny: have you got that, lad?

Clegg Aye.

Crosby   Good possession . . . If their hooker causes any trouble let *Walshy* bang his head.

Walsh   I already have done, lad. Don't worry.

They laugh.

Crosby   Cliff? Ought you want to add?

Owens   No. No. Mark your man. Don't wait for somebody else to take him.

Roar of the crowd off.

They look to **Thornton**, *who's been going round to individual players, nodding formally, advising, giving praise.*

Trevor *comes back in.*

Thornton   Good luck, lads. Keep at it. Don't let the pressure drop. Remember: it's thy advantage second half. Away from home, for them: it always tells.

Crosby   Aye . . .

Thornton   Good luck.

Players (*uninterested*)   Aye . . . thanks . . .

Thornton   Go up and shake them lads out o' the bloody boardroom, Mac . . . They'll watch the match from up theer if they get half a chance . . .

Mackendrick   Aye . . . Good luck, lads. Don't let up.

Players   No . . . Aye . . .

Mackendrick   See you after. Keep it up. Well done . . . (*On his way out.*) Well done . . . Well done, Trev. (*Slaps* **Trevor**'*s back as he goes.*)

Thornton *smiles round, nods at* **Crosby**, *then follows* **Mackendrick** *out.*

Crosby   Watch Tallon near your line.

Players (*Moving off*)   Aye . . . aye.

Owens   All right, then, lads. We're off . . .

Crosby   Barry . . .

Copley (*on move out, hands clenched*)   Aye.

Crosby   Are you listening . . .

Copley   Aye. Aye. Don't worry.

Crosby   Right, then . . . Fieldy: how's thy eye?

Fielding   All right.

Crosby   It's bloody well opened. (*To* **Luke**.) Look.

Fielding   Aye. Aye. It'll be all right. (*Dismisses it, goes.*)

Crosby   Remember . . . Fenny . . . Patsy . . .

Players (*filing out*)   Aye . . . aye . . . All right.

They go. **Crosby** *nods to each one at the door, advising, slapping backs.*

Luke *and* **Sandford** *start collecting the kit to take out.* **Moore** *and* **Spencer** *still in their track-suits, pick up a bucket and a bag between them, waiting to follow* **Crosby** *out after the players have gone.*

Roar of the crowd off as the players go out.

Harry *has come in to collect the towels, tapes, bottles, etc., left lying around.*

Luke (*packing his bag*)   See you out theer, Danny . . .

Crosby   Right . . . Frank . . . Billy?

Spencer   Aye.

Crosby   Right . . .

They go.

Sandford, Luke *and* **Harry** *are left.*

Luke   Well, then, Harry . . . How's t'a barn?

Harry   All right.

Luke   Been warming up in here, then, have you?

Harry   I bloody haven't.

Sandford (*warming hands at fire*)   I'm not so sure I wouldn't prefer it here meself.

Crowd roars off.

Ay up. Ay up. That's it. We're off. (*He zips up his track-suit top, pulls his scarf round his neck.*)

Luke   Be with you in a sec, old lad.

Sandford   All right. (*Goes.*)

Luke and **Harry** *work in silence for a moment.*

Luke   Do you ever back on matches, Harry?

Harry   What?

Luke   Bookies.

Harry   I don't.

Luke   Nor 'osses?

Harry   Nowt.

Luke   What do you do in your spare time, then?

Harry   I don't have any spare time.

Luke   What do you do when you're not up here, then?

Harry   I'm alus up here.

Luke   Sleep up here, then, do you?

Roar off. **Luke** *raises head, listens: packs his bag.*

Harry   I sleep at home.

Luke   Where's home?

Harry   Home's in our house. That's where home is.

Luke   A damn good place to have it, lad.

Harry   Bloody keep it theer, an' all.

Luke   Thornton here, then, was he: first half?

Harry   Aye.

Luke   Crafty . . . He'll never put himself out, you know, unduly.

Harry   And Mackendrick.

Luke   Where one goes his shadder follows.

Harry It's his place . . . He can do what he likes . . . He can sit in here the whole afternoon if he bloody likes.

Luke I suppose he can.

Roar off.

F'un him up here, you know, one night.

Harry What's that?

Luke Sir Frederick . . . Came back one night . . . Left me tackle . . . Saw a light up in the stand . . . Saw him sitting theer. Alone. Crouched up. Like that.

Harry His stand. Can sit theer when he likes.

Luke Ten o'clock at night.

Harry Ten o'clock i' the bloody morning. Any time he likes.

Luke *fastens his bag.*

Luke Is it true, then, what they say?

Harry What's that?

Luke Thy's never watched a match.

Harry Never.

Luke Why's that?

Harry My job's in here. Thy job's out yonder.

Luke They ought to set thee on a pair o' bloody rails. (*Goes over to the door.*)

Harry Most jobs you get: they're bloody nowt . . .

Luke *pauses at the door.*

Don't know what they work for . . .

Luke What?

Harry Not any more. Not like it was . . .

Luke Well, thy works for the bloody club.

Harry I work for Sir Frederick, lad: for nob'dy else.

Luke *looks across at him.*

I mun run the bloody bath. (*He goes.*)

Luke *watches from the door, then looks round for anything he's forgotten. Comes back in, gets scissors. Sound off, from the bath entrance, of running water. He crosses to the door and goes.*

Harry *comes back a moment later. He gets towels from the basket and lays them out on the bench, by each peg. At one point there's a roar and booing from the crowd, trumpets, rattles. It dies away to a fainter moan.* **Harry** *turns on the Tannoy.*

Tannoy (*accompanied by roaring of the crowd*) '. . . Copley . . . Clegg . . . Morley . . . Fenchurch! . . . inside . . . passes . . . Jagger . . . Stringer . . . Tackled. Fourth tackle. Scrum down. Walsh . . . Fielding . . . Walsh having words with his opposite number! Getting down. The scrum is just inside United's half . . . almost ten yards in from the opposite touch . . . put in . . . some rough play inside that scrum . . . Referee Tallon's blown up . . . free kick . . . no . . . scrum down . . . not satisfied with the tunnel . . . ball in . . . Walsh's head is up . . . (*Laughter.*) There's some rough business inside that scrum . . . my goodness! . . . Ball comes out . . . Morley . . . Copley . . . Owens . . . Owens to Trevor . . . *Trevor is going to drop a goal* . . . too late . . . He's left it far too late . . . They've tried that once before . . . Kendal . . . '

Harry *switches the Tannoy off.*

Great roar outside.

Harry *has crossed to the fire; more coal; pokes it. Goes off to the bath entrance.*

A moment later the door from the porch opens: **Sandford** *comes in.*

Sandford (*calling*) Luke? . . . Luke?

Harry (*re-emerging*) He's just gone . . .

Sandford Oh, Christ . . .

Harry Anything up?

Sandford Gone through the bloody tunnel . . . Missed him.

Roar increasing off. **Sandford** *hurries out.* **Harry** *stands in the centre of the room waiting. Baying of the crowd. A few moments later, voices off: 'Hold the bloody door.' 'This side.' 'This side.' 'Take his shoulder.' 'I'm all right. I'm all right. Don't worry.'*

The door opens: **Kendal** *comes in, supported by* **Crosby** *and* **Moore**.

Kendal   It's all right . . . It's bloody nowt . . . Where is it? Where's he put it?

Crosby   Get him down . . . no, over here. Over here. On this.

They take him to the massage table.

Kendal   Now, don't worry. Don't worry . . . Don't worry. I'll be all right . . .

Moore   S'all right, Kenny, lad. All right.

Crosby   Doesn't know where he is . . . Now, come on. Lie down, Kenny, lad. Lie down.

Kendal   S'all right. S'all right.

Crosby   Where's bloody Lukey . . . Frank: get us a bloody sponge. Harry: o'd him down.

Crosby *tries to hold* **Kendal** *down: having been laid on the table, he keeps trying to sit up.*

Harry *comes over to the table. He watches, but doesn't help.*

Harry (*to* **Moore**)   Over theer . . . that bucket.

Moore *goes off to the bath entrance.*

Crosby   Come on, Kenny. Come on . . . Lie down, lad.

Kendal   S'all right . . . S'all right . . . I'll go back on.

Crosby   You'll go nowhere, lad . . . Come on . . . Come on, then, Kenny, lad. Lie still. I want to bloody look . . . Come on . . .

The door opens: **Sandford** *comes in, followed by* **Luke** *with his bag.*

Luke How is he? . . . Don't move him . . . Let's have a look.

Crosby Where's thy been? . . . On thy bloody holidays, hast tha?

Luke Let's have a look . . . I was coming up . . .

Crosby Nose . . .

Steps back, **Sandford** *takes hold.*

Crosby *gets a towel, wipes his hands.*

Kendal Nose . . . It's me nose, Lukey . . .

Luke Lie still, lad, now. Lie still.

Kendal I can't bloody see, Lukey . . .

Luke Now just lie still . . . That's it . . . That's right . . .

Moore *has brought the sponge.*

Get some clean water, lad. That's no good . . .

Sandford Here . . . here . . . I'll get it. (*To* **Moore**.) Come round here. Get o'd o' this.

Moore *takes* **Sandford**'s *place.*

Sandford *goes off to bath entrance.*

Luke *has looked at* **Kendal**'s *wound.* **Kendal**'s *face is covered in blood.* **Luke** *sponges round his cheeks and mouth, then stoops down to his bag, gets out cotton wool.* **Kendal** *is still trying to get up.*

Moore It's all right, Kenny, lad. All right.

Kendal Can't see . . .

Luke Now just keep your eyes closed, lad . . . Harry: can you get a towel?

Moore   I don't think Ken wa' even looking . . . His bloody head came down . . . bloody boot came up . . .

Harry *has passed over a towel.* **Moore** *takes it.*

Luke   Shove it underneath his head . . . Kenny? Keep your head still, lad.

Sandford *has brought in a bowl of water.*

Luke *wipes away the blood with cotton wool, examines the damage.* **Sandford** *pours a drop of disinfectant from the bottle into the bowl of water.* **Luke** *dips in the cotton wool, wipes* **Kendal***'s nose.*

Crosby*, not really interested, having wiped the blood from his hands and his track-suit, looks on impatiently over* **Luke***'s back.*

Kendal   A bit o' plaster: I'll go back on.

Luke   Nay, lad. The game's over for you today.

Kendal   I'll be all right . . . I'll get back on . . .

Crosby   He's off, then, is he?

Luke   Aye . . .

Sandford   Aye . . . (*Gestures up.*) I'll take him up.

Crosby   Right . . . Frank. Come on. Not have you hanging about down here.

Sandford   Who you sending on?

Crosby (*looks round; to* **Frank**)   Do you think you can manage, then, out theer?

Moore   Aye!

Crosby   Come on, then. Let's have you up.

Moore*, quickly, jubilantly, strips off his track-suit.*

Lukey . . .

Luke   Aye.

Crosby   As soon as you've done. Let's have you up . . .
Kenny: do you hear that, lad?

Kendal (*half-rising*)   Aye . . .

Crosby   Well done, lad . . . Just do as Lukey says . . .

Kendal   Aye . . .

Crosby (*to* **Moore**)   Come on. Come on. Not ready yet . . .

Has gone to the door. **Moore** *scrambles out of the suit.* **Crosby** *goes.*
Moore, *flexing his legs, pulling down his jersey, etc., hesitates.*

He goes.

Luke   Theer, then, Kenny . . .

Luke *has finished washing the wound and has dressed it with a
plaster. He now helps* **Kendal** *up with* **Sandford**'s *assistance.*

If there's ought you want, just give a shout.

Kendal   There's me electric tool-kit, Luke . . .

Luke   I've got it here, old lad . . . Thy'll be all right . . .

Kendal   Fifteen quid that cost . . . just o'er . . .

Sandford   Here, then. Come on . . . Let's have you in the
bath. Come on. Come on, now . . . It wouldn't do you much
good if you dropped it in . . .

Kendal *has got up from the table.*

Sandford *helps him over to the bath entrance.*

Luke *finishes packing his bag.*

The porch door opens: **Mackendrick** *comes in.*

Mackendrick   How is he?

Luke   He'll be all right.

Mackendrick   Too bloody old, you know. If I've said it
once, I've said it . . .

Luke   Aye.

Mackendrick (*calls through*)   How're you feeling, Kenny, lad.

Kendal (*off*)   All right.

Mackendrick   All right, Sandy?

Sandford (*off*)   Aye. I'll have him in the bath.

Mackendrick   Taking him up . . . ? (*Gestures up.*)

Sandford (*off*)   Aye.

Mackendrick   I'll see about a car.

Sandford (*off*)   Shan't be long.

Mackendrick (*to* **Luke**)   I'll go up to the office.

Luke   Tool-kit. (*Shows him.*)

Mackendrick *looks in.*

Bloody shelves . . .

Mackendrick   Poor old Kenny . . .

Luke   Bloody wife.

Mackendrick   Like that, then, is it?

Luke   Been round half the teams i' the bloody league . . . one time or another. (*Packs his bag and goes over to the bath entrance.*) I'll get on up, then, Sandy, lad.

Sandford (*off*)   Aye.

Luke   Be all right, then, Kenny, lad?

Kendal (*off*)   Aye . . .

Luke *collects his bag.*

Luke   You'll see about a taxi, then?

Mackendrick   Aye.

Roar off.

They lift their heads.

Luke   Another score.

Mackendrick (*gestures at bath entrance*)   I'll get up and tell Sir Freddy, then.

Mackendrick *goes out by the office entrance,* **Luke** *by the porch.*

Harry *is left alone. He's cleared up the bits of cotton wool and lint; he collects the used towels.*

Sandford *brings in* **Kendal***'s used kit, drops it on the floor. Gets a towel.*

Sandford   Take care of that, then, Harry . . .

Harry   Aye.

Sandford   Them his clothes?

Harry   Aye.

Sandford *gets them down. He goes to the bath entrance with the towel.*

Sandford (*off*)   Come on, then, Kenny . . . Let's have you out.

Harry *retidies the massage table, resetting the head-rest which, for* **Kendal***'s sake, has been lowered.*

A moment later **Kendal***'s led in with a towel round him.*

Can you see ought?

Kendal   Bloody dots . . .

Sandford   No, this way, lad, then. Over here.

Kendal   Is the game over, Sandy . . . ?

Sandford   Just about. Sit theer. I'll get you dried . . .

Kendal *sits on the bench.* **Sandford** *dries his legs and feet, then he dries his head.*

Harry *looks on.*

Pass his shirt, then, will you?

Harry *passes* **Kendal***'s shirt and vest over.*

There's a roaring of the crowd off.

Kendal   Are we winning?

Sandford   Come on, then . . . Get your head in this.

Kendal   Can't remember . . .

Sandford *pulls his vest and shirt round his head.* **Kendal** *dazedly pushes in his arms.*

Harry   What's he done?

Sandford   Nose.

Harry   Bro'k it, has he?

Sandford   Aye.

Kendal   Remember shopping.

Sandford   We've got it here, old lad. Don't worry.

Kendal   Bloody fifteen quid . . .

Harry   F'ust one this year.

Sandford   Come on, then, lad . . . Let's have you up.

Sandford *helps* **Kendal** *to his feet.* **Harry** *watches, hands in pockets.* **Kendal** *leans on* **Sandford.** **Sandford** *pulls on his trousers.*

Harry   Three collar-bones we had one week . . . Two o' theirs . . . the last un ours . . . Ankle . . . Bloody thigh-bone, once . . . Red hair . . . He never played again.

Sandford (*to* **Kendal**)   Come on, come on, then, lad . . . o'd up.

Kendal   Steam-boilers, lad . . . Bang 'em in . . . Seen nothing like it. Row o' rivets . . . Christ . . . Can hardly see ought . . . Sandy?

Sandford   Here, old lad. Now just hold tight . . . Come on. Come on, now. Let's have you out of here . . . (*To* **Harry**.) Will you see if Mr Mackendrick's got that car? . . . (*As* **Harry** *goes*.) Harry: can you find me coat as well?

Harry *goes, stiffly, leaving by office entry.*

Roar off, rises to peak, applause, bugles, rattles.

Kendal *turns towards sound, as if to go.*

Nay, lad: can't go with nothing on your feet.

Sits **Kendal** *down, puts on his socks and shoes.*

Kendal (*dazed*)   Started lakin' here when I wa' fifteen, tha knows . . . Intermediates . . . Then I went out, on loan, to one of these bloody colliery teams . . . bring 'em up at the bloody weekend in bloody buckets . . . play a game o' bloody football . . . booze all Sunday . . . back down at the coalface Monday . . . Seen nothing like it. Better ring my wife.

Sandford   What?

Kendal   She won't know.

Sandford   She's not here today, then?

Kendal   No . . .

Sandford   I'll see about it, lad. Don't worry.

Kendal   If I'm bloody kept in, or ought . . .

Sandford   Aye. It'll be all right.

Kendal   The woman next door has got a phone.

Sandford   Aye. I'll see about it, lad. All right. (*Gets up.*) Let's have your coat on. Won't bother with your tie.

Kendal *stands.* **Sandford** *helps him into his raincoat.*

Kendal   I wa' going to get a new un . . . until I bought this drill . . .

Sandford   Aye! (*Laughs.*)

Kendal   Start saving up again . . .

Sandford   That's right.

Harry *comes in through the office door. He brings in* **Sandford**'s *overcoat.*

Harry   There's one outside already.

Sandford   Good.

Harry (*watches* **Sandford**'s *efforts*)   Alus one or two out theer.

Sandford   Yeh.

Harry   Sat'days.

Sandford   Could alus use Sir Frederick's, then.

Harry   Aye . . .

Sandford   How're you feeling, lad?

Kendal   All right.

Sandford   Come on, then, lad . . . Just fasten this . . .

Kendal *holds his head up so* **Sandford** *can fasten on the dressing Luke has left. It covers his nose and is fastened with plaster to his cheeks.*

Kendal   Is it broke?

Sandford   There's a bit of a gash, old lad.

Kendal   Had it broken once before . . .

Sandford   Can you manage to the car? (*Collects his coat.*)

Kendal   Wheer is it, then? (*Turns either way.*)

Sandford   Here it is, old lad . . . (*Hands him his parcel.*)

Kendal   Have to get some glasses . . . hardly see . . .

Sandford (*to* **Harry**)   Looks like bloody Genghis Khan . . . Come on, then, Kenny . . . Lean on me. (*To* **Harry**.) Still got me bloody boots on . . . I'll get them in the office . . . See you, lad.

Harry *watches them go.*

He waits. Then he picks up the used towel, takes it off to dump inside the bath entrance.

He comes back, looks round, switches on the Tannoy.

Tannoy (*crowd roar*)   ' . . . to Walsh . . . reaches the twenty-five . . . goes down . . . plays back . . . (*Roar.*) . . . Comes to

Clegg to Atkinson . . . Atkinson to the substitute Moore . . .
Moore in now, crashes his way through . . . goes down . . .
Walsh comes up . . . out to Owens . . . Owens through . . .
dummies . . . beautiful move . . . to Stringer, Stringer out to
Patsy . . . Patsy out to Trevor, who's come up on the wing
. . . kicks . . . Copley . . . Fenchurch . . . Fielding . . . *Morley*
. . . (*Roar.*) Ball bounces into touch . . . scrum . . . (*Pause, dull
roar.*) Growing dark now . . . ball goes in, comes out, Tallon
blows . . . free kick . . . scrum infringement . . . one or two
tired figures there . . . can see the steam, now, rising from
the backs . . . Trevor's running up and down, blowing in his
hands . . . Kick . . . good kick . . . (*Crowd roar.*) Finds touch
beyond the twenty-five . . . (*Crowd roar.*)

Harry *sits, listening.*

Fade: sound and light.

Act Three

The same.

Noise: shouting, singing, screeching, cries off. The Tannoy is playing music.

Patsy, *a towel round his waist, is drying himself with a second towel, standing by his clothes. He does it with the same care with which he prepared himself for the match.*

Harry *is picking up the mass of discarded shorts, jerseys, jock-straps, and putting them on the basket.*

A pile of towels stands on the rubbing-down table.

Spencer *is half-dressed in trousers and shirt, combing his wet hair in the mirror.*

Crosby *is going round checking boots, putting pairs together by the massage table to be collected up.*

Crosby (*to* **Spencer**)   Up there waiting for you, is she, Billy?

Spencer   Aye. All being well. (*Combing in mirror.*) Bloody expecting me to play today, an' all.

Crosby   Ne'er mind. Next week: might be in luck.

Spencer   Bloody away next week!

Crosby   Maybe she'll have to bloody travel.

Spencer   Not the travelling kind, you know.

Crosby   Can't win 'em all, old lad. Don't worry . . . (*Calls.*) Come on. Let's have you out o' there . . . (*Switches off Tannoy, moves on. To* **Patsy**.) How're you feeling, then, old lad?

Patsy   All right. Bit stiff. (*Winces: eases arm.*)

Crosby   How's thy shoulder?

Patsy   All right.

Crosby   Bloody lovely try. Worth any amount o' bloody knocks is that.

Patsy   Aye.

Crosby   Couple more next week . . . should be all right.

Patsy   Aye. (*Doesn't respond, drying himself, turns to check his clothes.*)

Jagger *comes bursting in from the bath.*

Jagger   Dirty bugger . . . dirty sod . . . Danny: go bloody stop him. (*Snatches towel, rubs his hair vigorously.*) Walshy – pittling in the bloody bath.

Spencer (*calling through*)   Thy'll have to disinfect that bloody water . . . (*Laughing.*)

Walsh (*off*)   This *is* disinfectant, lad.

Crosby   Come on, Walshy: let's have you out . . .

Takes a towel and dries **Jagger**'s *back.*

Jagger   Dirty bugger: dirty sod!

Walsh (*off*)   Come on, Jagger. You could do with a bloody wash.

Jagger   Not in that, you dirty sod . . . Set bloody Patsy onto you, if you don't watch out.

Water comes in from the bath.

Dirty! Dirty! . . .

Dances out of the way: laughter and shouting off.

Crosby   Come on, Trevor. Teach 'em one or two manners, then . . . Bloody college-man . . . going to go away disgusted with all you bloody working lads.

Another jet of water. **Crosby** *lurches out of the way.*

Bloody well be in there if you don't watch out.

Jeers, cries.

Copley (*off*)   Too bloody old!

Clegg (*off*)   Come on, Danny. Show us what you've got.

Crosby Get summat here that'll bloody well surprise you,
lad . . .

Laughter, cries.

And you!

Laughter off.

Sithee . . . Billy. Go in and quieten 'em down.

Spencer Nay . . . gotten out in one bloody piece. Not
likely. Send Harry in. He'll shift 'em out.

Harry *looks up: they laugh. He doesn't respond.*

Singing starts off, then all join in from the bath.

Luke *comes in.*

Crosby Got through, then, did you?

Luke He'll be all right . . .

Jagger Kenny?

Luke Broken nose.

Jagger Keeping him in, then, are they?

Luke Aye.

Jagger Give his missus chance to bloody roam.

Luke (*goes over to* **Patsy**) How's it feel, old lad?

Patsy All right. (*Eases his shoulder, stiffly.*)

Luke Come in tomorrow: I'll give you a bloody rub.

Patsy Right.

Luke Need a drop of stuff on theer. (*Goes to his bag.*)

Trevor *has come in, wiping himself down with a towel.*

Trevor Just look . . . just beginning to get up
circulation . . .

Flexes his fingers.

Jagger Circulate a bit lower down for me.

Crosby *has a towel and now dries* **Trevor***'s back.*

Trevor Bloody shaking, still. Just look. (*Holds out his hands, trembling.*)

Crosby Don't worry. This time tomorrow . . .

Flicks towel to **Spencer**, *who finishes rubbing* **Trevor**'s *back.*

Spencer What's thy teach, then, Trev?

Trevor Mathematics.

Spencer Maths . . .

Trevor One of your subjects, is it?

Spencer One . . . (*Laughs.*)

Luke T'other's bloody lasses, Trev.

Spencer Nay, I gi'e time o'er to one or two other things, an' all.

They laugh.

Jagger Here . . . Got the two-thirty, Lukey, have you?

Luke Somewheer . . . (*Tosses the paper over from his pocket.*)

Spencer (*to* **Trevor**) That kind o' mathematics, Trev.

Slaps **Trevor**'s *back: finished drying.*

Trevor Shoulda known. (*Turns away to get dressed.*)

Jagger Let me see . . . (*Examines stop-press.*) One-thirty . . . (*To* **Spencer**.) Quite a bit fastened up in that . . . (*Reading.*) Two o'clock . . . Two-thirty . . . No . . .

Crosby What's that, Jagger, lad?

Jagger *tosses paper down. Goes to his clothes.*

Spencer Let's have a look.

Jagger (*to* **Luke**) Don't say a word to bloody Walsh.

Luke Shan't say a word. (*Laughs.*) Not a sausage.

Luke *has dabbed an orange-staining antiseptic on* **Patsy**'s *arm; now he crosses to* **Trevor***. As* **Trevor** *starts to dress he moves round him, dabbing on antiseptic with cotton wool.*

Hold still. Hold still.

Clegg *comes in, drying.*

Clegg   Bit lower down there, Lukey.

Luke   Aye. (*Laughs.*)

Spencer (*reading*)   Bloody Albatross. Seven to one.

Jagger   What d'you back, Billy, lad?

Spencer   Same as you, Jag. Little Nell. (*To* **Luke**.) Tipped the bloody 'oss himself.

Jagger   Bloody Walsh . . . Never hear the end.

Clegg   What's that?

Jagger*, dry, has started to dress.* **Spencer** *has taken the towel from* **Clegg** *and is drying his back.*

Jagger   Albatross: come up . . . (*Gestures off.*)

Clegg (*to* **Spencer**)   What's that?

Spencer   I'm saying nowt.

Flicks the towel to **Clegg***, picks up another.*

Copley *has come in, followed by* **Fenchurch. Spencer** *goes to dry* **Copley**'s *back,* **Crosby** *to dry* **Fenchurch**'s*.*

Copley   Sithee, there ought to be a special bloody bath for those dirty bloody buggers: I'm muckier now than when I bloody well went in.

Walsh (*off, siren-call*)   Barry! Barry! *We can't do without you, Barry!*

Copley (*calling*)   Sod off.

Morley (*siren, off*)   *Barr . . . y!*

Walsh (*siren, off*)   Barr . . . y . . .

Morley (*off*)   Barr . . . y! . . . We're *waiting,* Barry!

Copley (*calling*)   Piss off!

Crosby   Come on, Fieldy . . . Keep those ignorant sods in line.

Fielding (*off*)   I'm in the bloody shower. I'm not in with those mucky bloody sods.

Jagger   How're you feeling, Fenny, lad?

Fenchurch   All right . . . (*Indicating paper.*) Results in theer, then, are they?

Clegg (*has picked it up to read*)   Aye. (*Reads.*) 'Latest score: twelve-seven.' Patsy: they didn't get thy try . . . Sithee: pricked up his bloody ears at that.

They laugh. **Patsy**, *having turned, goes back to dressing.*

Fenchurch   Fifteen-seven . . .

Jagger   Fifteen-seven.

Fenchurch   Put a good word in with Sir Frederick, then.

Crosby   Good word about bloody what, then, lad?

Fenchurch   Me and Jagger, Danny boy . . . Made old Patsy's bloody try . . . In't that right, then, Jagger lad?

Patsy   Made me own bloody try. Ask Jack . . .

Stringer *has come in, shaking off water.* **Crosby** *goes to him with a towel: dries his back.*

Morley (*off*)   Any more for any more?

Laughter off.

Walsh (*off*)   Barry . . . y! *We're waiting, Barry!*

Fenchurch   Take no notice. Silly sod.

Stringer   Where's Cliff, then?

Jagger   Up in the directors' bath, old lad.

Stringer   Is that right, then?

Crosby   Captain's privilege, lad.

Stringer Bloody hell . . . (*Snatches towel, goes over to the bench to dry himself.*)

Luke *is still going round, dabbing on antiseptic.*

Luke Any cuts, bruises: ought that needs fastening up?

Jagger I've a couple of things here that need a bit of bloody attention, Lukey . . .

Luke What's that?

Goes over; **Jagger** *shows him.*

They all laugh.

Patsy *has crossed to the mirror to comb his hair.*

Patsy Did you see a young woman waiting for me up there, Danny?

Groans and jeers from the players.

Clegg How do you do it, Patsy? I can never make that out.

Fenchurch Nay, his girl-friend's a bloody schoolmistress. Isn't that right, then, Patsy?

Patsy *doesn't answer: combs his hair, straightens his tie.*

Jagger Schoolmistress?

Fenchurch Teaches in Trevor's bloody school . . . Isn't that right, then, Trev?

Trevor *nods, doesn't look up: gets on with his dressing.*

Jagger What do you talk about, then, Patsy?

They laugh. **Patsy** *is crossing to his coat. With some care he pulls it on.*

Clegg (*having gone to him*) The moon in *June* . . . Is coming out quite *soon*!

Walsh (*off*) Barr . . . y! *Where are you, Barr . . . y!*

Copley Piss off, you ignorant sod.

Morley (*off*) Barr . . . y! *We're waiting, Barr . . . y!*

Laughter off.

Luke   Sithee . . . Can you sign these autograph books:
there's half a dozen lads outside . . . Clean forgot. (*Takes them
from his pocket, puts them on the table.*)

Jagger   By God: just look at that!

Patsy *has already crossed to the table.*

Pen out in a bloody flash . . .

Patsy *takes out a pen clipped to his top pocket. Writes.* **Jagger**
stoops over his shoulder to watch.

He can write, an' all . . . 'Patrick Walter Turner.' Beautiful.
Bloody beautiful is that.

Patsy   Piss off.

Jagger   Here, now. Bloody language, Trev! . . . Hears that,
she'll never speak again.

Fenchurch   Put you down in her bloody book . . .

Jagger   Black mark.

Fenchurch   A thousand lines . . .

Jagger   'I must not bloody swear, you cunt.'

They laugh.

Fielding *comes in, picks up a towel.* **Spencer** *goes over to dry his
back.*

Fielding   They're going to be in theer a bloody fo'tnight
. . . Harry – go in and pull that bloody plug.

Harry   Aye. (*Doesn't look up.*)

*Burst of laughter. Shouts off: 'Give over! Give over! You rotten bloody
sod!'*

Stringer   They could do with putting in separate bloody
showers in theer.

Crosby   What's that, Jack?

Stringer   Separate showers. It's not hygienic, getting bathed together.

Clegg   It's not. He's right. That's quite correct.

Fenchurch   Put a bit o' colour in your cheeks, old lad.

Stringer   I've got all the colour theer I need.

Jagger   Played a grand game today, though, Jack. (*Winks at the others.*)

Stringer   Aye. (*Mollified.*)

Jagger   Marvellous. Bloody fine example, that.

Stringer   Aye. Well . . . I did my best.

Jagger   Them bloody forwards: see them clear a way.

They laugh. **Stringer** *dries his hair, rubbing fiercely.*

Atkinson *comes in from the bath, limping.*

Crosby *gets a towel, dries his back.*

Luke   Let's have you on here, Bryan. Let's have a look.

Luke *waits by the table while* **Atkinson** *gets dry.*

Morley (*off*)   Barry! Where are you, Barry!

Walsh (*off*)   Barry! *We're waiting, Barry . . .*

Copley *looks round: sees one of the buckets: takes it to the bath entrance: flings the cold water in.*

Cries and shouts off.

The players laugh.

Crosby   Go on. Here . . . Here's a bloody 'nother.

Copley *takes it, flings the water in.*

Cries, shouts off.

The players laugh, looking over at the bath entrance.

Atkinson *is dry now and, with a towel round him, he lies down on the massage table.* **Luke** *examines his leg.*

Patsy, *having got on his coat, has returned to the mirror. Final adjustments: collar, tie, hair . . .*

Stringer *continues getting dressed.* **Trevor** *joins* **Patsy** *at the mirror.*

Fenchurch, Jagger *and* **Clegg** *are almost dressed,* **Fielding** *just beginning.*

Jagger   Go on, Barry! Ought else you've bloody got!

Copley *looks round, sees nothing.*

Crosby   Here . . . Come on . . . Turn on that bloody hose.

He picks up the end of the hose by the bath entrance, turns the tap. They spray the water into the bath entrance.

Cries and shouts from the bath.

The players call out: 'More! More! Go on! All over!'

Cries and shouts off. A moment later **Moore** *and* **Morley** *come running in, shaking off water, the players scattering.*

Moore   Give over! Give over! Ger off!

They grab towels, start rubbing down.

Walsh (*off*)   More! More! Lovely! Lovely! . . . That's it, now, lads . . . No. No. Right . . . Lovely. Lovely . . . Bit lower, Barry . . . Lovely! Grand!

The players laugh.

Crosby (*to* **Copley**)   All right . . .

Luke   That's enough . . .

Crosby   Nowt'll get through that bloody skin, I can tell you. (*Calls through.*) We're putting the lights out in ten minutes, lad . . . You can stay there all night if tha bloody wants.

Copley *turns off the tap.*

The players go back to getting dressed.

Stringer   All over me bloody clothes. Just look.

Fielding   Here . . . here, old lad. I'll mop it up . . . Grand game today, then, Jack.

Stringer   Aye . . . All right.

Crosby *dries* **Moore**'s *back*, **Spencer** *dries* **Morley**'s.

Crosby   What's it feel like, Frank?

Moore   Grand . . . Just got started.

Fielding   Knows how to bloody lake, does Frank . . . ten minutes . . .

Moore   Nearer thi'ty.

Fielding   Just time to get his jersey mucky . . .

Crosby   He'll bloody show you lads next week . . .

Fielding   Can't bloody wait to see, old lad.

Walsh (*off*)   Barry . . . *I'm waiting*, Barry!

The players laugh.

Copley   Well, I'm bloody well not waiting here for thee!

They laugh.

The door from the office has opened.

Thornton, *followed by* **Mackendrick**, *comes in.*

Thornton   Well done, lads . . . Bloody champion . . . well done . . . They'll not come here again in a bloody hurry . . . not feel half so bloody pleased . . . How's thy feeling, Patsy, lad?

Patsy   All right, sir.

Thornton   Lovely try . . . Bloody textbook, lad . . . Hope they got that down on bloody film . . . Frank? How's it feel, young man?

Moore   Pretty good. All right.

Crosby   Just got started . . .

Fielding   Just got into his stride, Sir Frederick.

Thornton   Another ten minutes . . . he'd have had a bloody try.

They laugh.

Set 'em a bloody fine example, lad, don't worry. Well played there, lad. Well done.

Mackendrick   Well done, lad.

Thornton   How's your leg, then, Bryan?

Atkinson   Be all right.

Atkinson *is still on the table.* **Luke** *is massaging the leg with oil.*

Thornton   Nasty bloody knock was that.

Atkinson   Went one way . . . Me leg went t'other.

Thornton (*to* **Trevor**)   How's your hands now, then, lad?

Trevor   All right. Fine, thanks. (*Has pulled on his club blazer. Looks up from dusting it down.*)

Thornton (*to* **Fielding**)   I hope you're going to get your eye seen to there, old lad.

Fielding   Aye.

Thornton   Bad news about old Kenny.

Players   Aye . . .

Walsh (*off*)   Barr . . . y . . . I am *waiting*, Barry!

Thornton   Who's that, then? Bloody Walsh?

Crosby   Aye.

Thornton (*going to the bath entrance*)   And who's thy waiting for, then, Walshy?

Pause.

Walsh (*off*)   Oh, good evening, Sir Frederick . . .

Thornton   I'll give you Sir bloody Frederick . . . I'll be inside that bath in a bloody minute.

Walsh (*off*)   Any time, Sir Frederick, any time is good enough for me.

The players laugh.

Mackendrick *has moved off amongst the players, going first to* **Patsy**, *then to* **Trevor**, *slapping backs: 'Well done. Good match.'*

Thornton *turns back to the players.*

Thornton   I think we ought to charge Walsh bloody rent: spends more time here than he does at home.

Crosby   Thy had five quid off him here last week: swearing to the referee.

Mackendrick   That's right. We did!

They laugh.

Thornton   No luck this week, then, I fancy?

Crosby   Shouldn't think so. Tallon's not above bloody answering back.

Thornton   Shifty bugger is old Walshy . . . Grand try in the first half, Mic. Good game.

Morley   Thanks.

Morley, *his back dried by* **Spencer**, *is now getting dressed.*

Thornton   Bloody well stuck to you in the second half, I noticed.

Morley   Aye . . . Hardly room to move about.

Thornton   Was Kenny's an accident, then . . . Or someb'dy catch him?

Morley   A bit slow, I think, today.

Atkinson   Too cold . . .

Morley   It went right through you.

Thornton   There's a bloody frost out theer already . . .
Shouldn't be surprised if it snows tonight . . . Jagger: grand
game, lad. Well done.

Jagger   Thanks, Sir Frederick.

Thornton   Shook their centre a time or two, I saw.

Jagger   Always goes off the bloody left foot.

Thornton   So I noticed . . . (*To* **Stringer**.) Well done there,
Jack. Well played.

Stringer   Thanks, Sir Frederick.

Thornton   One of your best games for a long time, lad . . .
Not that the others haven't been so bad. (*Laughs.*) Liked your
tackling. Stick to it . . . Low, low!

Stringer   Aye! That's right!

Thornton   Any knocks, bruises?

Stringer   No. No. Be all right.

Thornton   Come up tomorrow if you're feeling stiff. Lukey
here'll be doing his stuff.

Luke   Aye . . . That's right.

He slaps **Atkinson** *who gets up and starts to dress.*

Gi'e us a couple o' hours i' bed . . . mek it ten o'clock, old
lad.

After wiping his hands **Luke** *starts to check his bottles, cotton wool,
etc., packing them in his bag.*

Thornton   Bloody gossip shop is this on a Sunday morning
. . . Isn't that right, then, Mac?

Mackendrick   Aye. It is.

Patsy   I'll . . . er . . . get off, then, Sir Frederick . . . See you
next week, then, all being well.

Thornton   Your young lady waiting, is she?

Patsy   Aye . . . I think so.

Thornton   Grand game. Well done.

Patsy Thanks, Sir Frederick . . . See you next week, Mr Mackendrick.

Mackendrick Aye. Aye. Well done, young man.

Patsy Bye, lads!

Players (*without much interest*)   Aye . . . bye . . . cheerio.

Morley Gi'e her a big kiss, then, Patsy, lad.

Chorus of laughter.

Jagger Gi'e her one for me, an' all.

Fenchurch And me.

Copley And me.

Fielding And me.

Atkinson And me.

Clegg And me.

Moore And me.

Spencer And me, an' all.

They laugh.

Patsy *goes: leaves through the porch entrance.*

Mackendrick Bloody good example there is Pat . . . Saves his bloody money . . . Not like some.

Clegg Saves it for bloody what, though, Mac?

Mackendrick He's got some bloody brains has Pat . . . puts it i' the bank, for one . . .

Fielding Big-headed sod.

Crosby What's that?

Luke He's got some good qualities has Pat.

Fielding I don't know where he keeps them, then.

They laugh.

Thornton (*to* **Mackendrick**)   Nay, don't look at me, old lad. (*Laughs. Has gone over to the fire to warm his hands.*)

Jagger (*calling*)   Sing us a song, then, Jack, old love.

Stringer   Sing a bloody song thysen.

They laugh.

Owens *has come in from the office, dressed in a smart suit: a neat, cheerful, professional man.*

Owens   Look at this. Bloody opening-time. Not even dressed.

Morley   Where's thy been, then, Cliff?

Jagger   Up in Sir Frederick's private shower-room, have you?

Owens   I thought it might be crowded, lads, today. What with that and the bloody cold . . . (*Winks, crosses to the massage table. Loudly.*) Got a bit o' plaster, have you, Lukey?

Players   Give over! Give over! Get off!

Owens   Got a little cut here . . .

Players   Give over! Give over! Get off!

Owens, *winking, goes over to the fire to warm his hands.*

Jagger   Give him a bloody kiss, Sir Frederick . . . that's all he bloody wants.

They laugh.

Walsh *appears at the bath entrance, a towel around his middle. He stands in the bath entrance, nodding, looking in.*

Walsh   I thought I could hear him . . . (*To* **Owens**.) Come to see the workers, have you? How long're you going to give us, lad?

Owens   I'll give thee all the time thy wants, old love.

The others laugh.

Walsh (*gestures back*)   I've been waiting for you, Barry . . .

The others laugh.

Fenchurch What's thy want him for, then, Walsh?

Crosby What's he after, Barry? What's he want?

Walsh He knows what I've been waiting for.

They laugh.

Luke We're bloody well closing shop in a couple o' minutes, Walsh. You want to hurry up. You'll be turned out without thy bloody clothes.

Atkinson T'only bloody bath he gets is here.

They laugh. **Walsh** *still stands there, gazing in, confronted.*

Copley Come on, then, Walshy. Show us what you've got.

Walsh I'll show thee bloody nowt, old lad. (*Moves over towards his clothes.*) Keeping me bloody waiting . . . sat in theer.

They laugh.

I was *waiting* for you, Barry . . .

They laugh.

Clegg Come on, then, Walshy, lad . . .

Fenchurch Gi'e us a bloody shock.

Morley Mr Mackendrick, here: he's been hanging on for hours.

They laugh.

Mackendrick Nay, don't bring me into it, old lad. I've seen all of Walshy that I bloody want.

Walsh, *with great circumspection, the towel still around him, has started to put on his clothes: vest and shirt.*

Walsh Tell my bloody wife about you, Jagger . . . Dirty bloody sod . . .

Crosby (*to all of them*) Come on, come on, then. Let's have you out . . .

Harry (*entering*) Have you all finished, then, in theer?

Most of the players now are dressed; one or two have started to smoke.
Owens *and* **Thornton** *stand with their backs to the fire, looking
on.*

Harry *has collected up the jerseys, stockings, shorts and towels. He's
worked anonymously, overlooked, almost as if, for the players, he
wasn't there. Having taken out some of the boots, he comes back in.*

Walsh What?

Harry Have you finished with that bath?

Walsh What do you want me to bloody do? Sup the bloody
stuff, old lad?

They laugh.

Harry I'll go and empty it, then.

Fenchurch Mind how you touch that water, lad.

Fielding Bloody poisonous, is that.

Harry, *without any response, goes to the hose, takes it in to the bath,
reappears, turns the tap, goes off to the bath.*

Tallon *has put his head in from the office entrance. He's dressed in
an overcoat and scarf, and carries a small hold-all.*

Tallon Just say goodnight, then, lads.

Players Aye . . . aye . . . Goodnight . . . Goodnight . . .

Tallon A good game, lads.

Crosby Aye.

Tallon Both sides played very well. And in very difficult
conditions, too.

Crosby Aye. Aye. That's right.

Tallon Sorry about Kendal . . . I hear they've taken him
off.

Luke Aye . . . He'll be all right.

Tallon Keeping him in, then, are they?

Mackendrick Aye. That's right.

Tallon Say goodnight, then, Mr Mackendrick . . . See you soon.

Crosses, shakes hands with **Mackendrick**.

Mackendrick I don't think you've met Sir Frederick.

Tallon No. No. I haven't.

Thornton Admired your refereeing very much.

Tallon Thank you. Thank you very much, sir.

Thornton See you up here again, then, soon, I hope.

Tallon Aye. Aye. Our job, though, you never know.

Thornton If you bring the same result with you, you can come up every bloody week, tha knows.

They laugh.

Going upstairs, then, are you? (*Mimes drink.*)

Tallon No. No. I've to catch me train. Otherwise I would. This weather. You can never chance your luck . . . Well, goodbye. It's been a pleasure.

Nods to **Owens**, *ducks his head to the others, goes.*

Walsh Anybody heard the bloody two-thirty?

Jagger No.

Fenchurch No.

Spencer No.

Luke No.

Fielding No.

Moore No.

Walsh (*back to them, getting dressed*) By God, sunk me bloody week's wages theer . . . You haven't got a paper, Mac?

Mackendrick No. No. Haven't had a chance.

Copley Let's see. Now here's one . . . What wa're it, now?

Walsh (*dressing*) Two-thirty.

Copley (*reading*)   'One o'clock . . . one-thirty . . . two o'clock
. . . two-fifteen . . .'

Walsh   Come on, come on, come on . . .

Jagger *points it out.*

Copley   Two-thirty! . . . Let's see now. What d'thy bet?

Walsh   Just tell us the bloody winner. Come on. Come on.

Copley   What's this, now? . . . Can't see without me glasses
. . . Little . . . what is it?

Walsh   Oh, God.

Copley   Nell.

Walsh   Hell fire . . . Can't bloody well go home tonight.

Copley (*still reading*)   Worth having something on, was that.

Walsh   Tell bloody Jagger: don't tell me.

Jagger   And Fenny. (*Winking.*)

Walsh   And Fenny . . . Here. Let's have a look.

They wait, watching, suppressing their laughter as **Walsh***, eyes
screwed up, shortsighted, reads.*

Here! . . . Here! . . . What's this . . . (*Eyes screwed, still reads.*)

They burst out laughing.

Just look at that. Bloody Albatross! *Seven to one!*

Shows it to **Atkinson** *to be confirmed.*

Atkinson   That's right.

Walsh   I've won, I've won.

Embraces **Stringer***, who's standing near him, fastening his coat.*

Stringer   Go on. Go on. Ger off!

The players laugh.

Walsh   By God. That's made my bloody day, has that.

Mackendrick   More interested in that than he is in bloody
football.

Walsh   I am. I am, old lad . . . More bloody brass in this for a bloody start. (*Laughs, finishes his dressing.*) By God, then: see old Barry now . . . Wish thy'd washed my bloody back, then, don't you?

Copley   I think I bloody do. That's right.

They laugh.

Fielding   Well, then, lads. I'm off . . .

Players   See you, Fieldy . . . Bye.

Luke   Watch that bloody eye.

Fielding   Aye. Aye. It'll be all right.

Thornton   Bye, Fieldy. Well done, lad.

Fielding   Aye . . . (*Goes.*)

Jagger   Fenny . . . Ar' t'a barn, then? . . . Trev?

Fenchurch (*packing his bag*)   Aye . . .

Trevor   Aye.

Walsh   Lukey . . . where's my bloody cigar, old lad!

They laugh. **Luke** *gets out the cigar.*

Jagger *and* **Trevor** *have gone to the door. They're joined by* **Fenchurch** *carrying his bag.*

Jagger   See you, lads, then.

All   Aye.

Trevor   Bye.

All   Bye . . . See you.

Mackendrick   Well done, Trevor, lad.

Trevor   Aye . . .

They go.

Walsh *is lighting up.*

Thornton (*going*)   Mind you don't choke on that, then, Walshy.

Walsh   Don't bloody worry . . . From now on . . . Trouble free! (*Blows out a cloud of smoke for his amusement.*)

Thornton   Bye, lads . . . Clifford?

Owens   Aye. Shan't be a minute.

Thornton   Time for a snifter, lads, tha knows . . . (*Gestures up.*)

All   Aye . . .

Copley   Bye, Sir Frederick . . .

Thornton *goes through the office entrance.* **Mackendrick**, *nodding, follows.*

Crosby, *picking up a couple of remaining boots, goes off through the bath entrance.*

Stringer   Well, I've got everything, I think. I'm off.

Copley   Enjoyed yourself today, then, Jack?

Stringer   Aye. All right.

Clegg   They tell me your mother was here this afternoon, then, Jack.

Stringer   As likely.

Copley   T'only bloody fan he's got.

Stringer   I've got one or two more, an' all.

They laugh.

Atkinson   Give you a lift into town, Jack, if you like.

Stringer   No . . . no . . . I like to walk. (*He goes.*)

They laugh.

Walsh   Here . . . Here you are, then, Cliff.

Walsh, *having finished dressing, adjusted his buttonhole and combed his hair in the mirror, gets out another cigar. The others watch in amazement.*

Owens Thanks, Walshy . . . Thanks very much . . . Won't smoke it now. (*Smells it appreciatively.*)

Walsh Save it.

Owens Appreciate it later.

Walsh Not like these ignorant bloody sods . . .

Copley Well, bloody hell . . .

Walsh Come today, tha knows . . . All gone tomorrer.

Clegg Bloody hell.

Copley The stingy bugger . . .

Walsh *laughs: a last look round: coat.*

Crosby *comes back in through bath entrance.*

Crosby Come on. Come on. Let's have you out. (*Claps his hands.*)

Clegg A bloody fistful . . .

Walsh Just one. Just one. (*Puffs at his own.*) Just the odd one, old son.

Copley Greasing round the bloody captain, Danny.

Walsh Keep in wi' me bloody captain. Never know when you might need a bloody favour. Isn't that right, then, Cliff?

Owens That's right.

They laugh, going.

Atkinson Well, then, Walshy . . . (*Gestures up.*) Gonna buy us one?

Walsh I might . . .

They've moved over to the office door, except for **Owens, Crosby** *and* **Luke**.

Moore *stands to one side.*

Barry here, o' course, will have to do without . . . (*To* **Crosby**.) Never came when I bloody called . . . As for the rest . . . I might stand a round . . . Might afford it . . . And one for thee, old lad. All right?

Spencer   All right.

Walsh (*looking back*)   What was Jagger's horse, now?

Luke   Little Nell.

Walsh   Little Nell! (*He laughs.*)

Clegg   Are you coming, Frank?

Moore   Aye. Aye. I will.

Walsh (*to* **Moore**)   Thy's kept bloody quiet, old lad . . .

Moore   Aye . . .

Walsh   Don't let these bloody lads upset you.

Moore   No. No. (*Laughs.*)

Walsh (*puts his arm round* **Moore**'s *shoulder, going*)   Sithee, Barry . . . first flush o' bloody success is that.

Copley (*leaving*)   Mic?

Morley   Aye. Just about.

They go, laughing. Burst of laughter and shouts outside.

Silence. **Luke** *has packed his bag; he zips it up.* **Crosby** *is picking up the rest of the equipment: odd socks, shirts.*

Owens *gets out a cigarette; offers one to* **Crosby** *who takes one, then offers one to* **Luke** *who shakes his head.*

There's a sound of **Harry** *singing off: hymn.*

Owens *flicks a lighter. Lights* **Crosby**'s *cigarette, then his own.*

Crosby   Not two bloody thoughts to rub together . . . (*Gestures off.*) Walshy.

Owens   No. (*Laughs.*)

Crosby   Years ago . . . ran into a bloody post . . . out yonder . . . split the head of any other man . . . Gets up:

looks round: says, 'By God', then . . . 'Have they teken him off?'

They laugh. **Luke** *swings down his bag.*

Luke   I'm off.

Crosby   See you, Lukey.

Luke   Cliff . . .

Owens   Thanks, Lukey.

Luke (*calls*)   Bye, Harry . . .

They wait. Hymn continues.

Crosby   Wandered off . . . (*Taps his head: indicates* **Harry** *off.*)

Luke   Aye . . . See you, lads. (*Collects autograph books.*)

Owens   Bye, Lukey.

Luke *goes with his bag through the porch entrance.*

Crosby *picks up the last pieces. Hymn finishes.*

Crosby   How're you feeling?

Owens   Stiff.

Crosby   Bloody past it, lad, tha knows.

Owens   Aye. One more season, I think: I'm finished.

Crosby *laughs.*

Been here, tha knows, a bit too long.

Crosby   Nay, there's nob'dy else, old lad . . .

Owens   Aye . . . (*Laughs.*)

Crosby   Need thee a bit longer to keep these lads in line.

Owens   Aye. (*Laughs.*)

Crosby   Did well today.

Owens   They did. That's right.

Crosby   Bloody leadership, tha see, that counts.

Owens (*laughs*)   Aye . . .

Crosby (*calls through to bath*)   Have you finished, then, in theer . . .

No answer.

(*To* **Owens**.) Ger up yonder . . .

Owens   Have a snifter . . .

Crosby   Another bloody season yet.

Puts out the light.

Poor old Fieldy.

Owens   Aye.

Crosby   Ah, well . . . this time tomorrer.

Owens   Have no more bloody worries then.

They laugh. **Crosby** *puts his arm round* **Owens**. *They go.*
Pause.

Harry *comes in, looks round. He carries a sweeping brush. Starts sweeping. Picks up one or two bits of tape, etc. Turns on the Tannoy: light music.*

Sweeps.

The remaining light and the sound of the Tannoy slowly fade.

Curtain.

ROYAL COURT WRITERS

The Royal Court Writers Series was launched in 1981 to celebrate 25 years of the English Stage Company and 21 years since the publication of the first Methuen Modern Play. Published to coincide with each production, the series fulfils the dual role of programme and playscript.

The Royal Court Writers Series includes work by

Karim Alrawi	Terry Johnson
Thomas Babe	Manfred Karge
Sebastian Barry	Charlotte Keatley
Neil Bartlett	Paul Kember
Aphra Behn	Hanif Kureishi
Howard Brenton	Stephen Lowe
Jim Cartwright	David Mamet
Anton Chekhov	Mariane Mayer
Caryl Churchill	G. F. Newman
Sarah Daniels	Wallace Shawn
George Farquhar	Sam Shepard
John Guare	David Storey
Iain Heggie	Sue Townsend
Robert Holman	Timberlake Wertenbaker
Ron Hutchinson	Snoo Wilson

Methuen Modern Plays

include work by

Jean Anouilh
John Arden
Margaretta D'Arcy
Peter Barnes
Brendan Behan
Edward Bond
Bertolt Brecht
Howard Brenton
Simon Burke
Jim Cartwright
Caryl Churchill
Noël Coward
Sarah Daniels
Nick Dear
Shelagh Delaney
David Edgar
Dario Fo
Michael Frayn
Paul Godfrey
John Guare
Peter Handke
Jonathan Harvey
Declan Hughes
Terry Johnson
Barrie Keeffe
Stephen Lowe

Doug Lucie
John McGrath
David Mamet
Patrick Marber
Arthur Miller
Mtwa, Ngema & Simon
Tom Murphy
Peter Nichols
Joseph O'Connor
Joe Orton
Louise Page
Luigi Pirandello
Stephen Poliakoff
Franca Rame
Philip Ridley
David Rudkin
Willy Russell
Jean-Paul Sartre
Sam Shepard
Wole Soyinka
C. P. Taylor
Theatre de Complicite
Theatre Workshop
Sue Townsend
Timberlake Wertenbaker
Victoria Wood

For a Complete Catalogue of
Methuen Drama titles

write to:

Methuen Drama
Michelin House
81 Fulham Road
London SW3 6RB